Damone's Abstract Coloring Book

volume 6

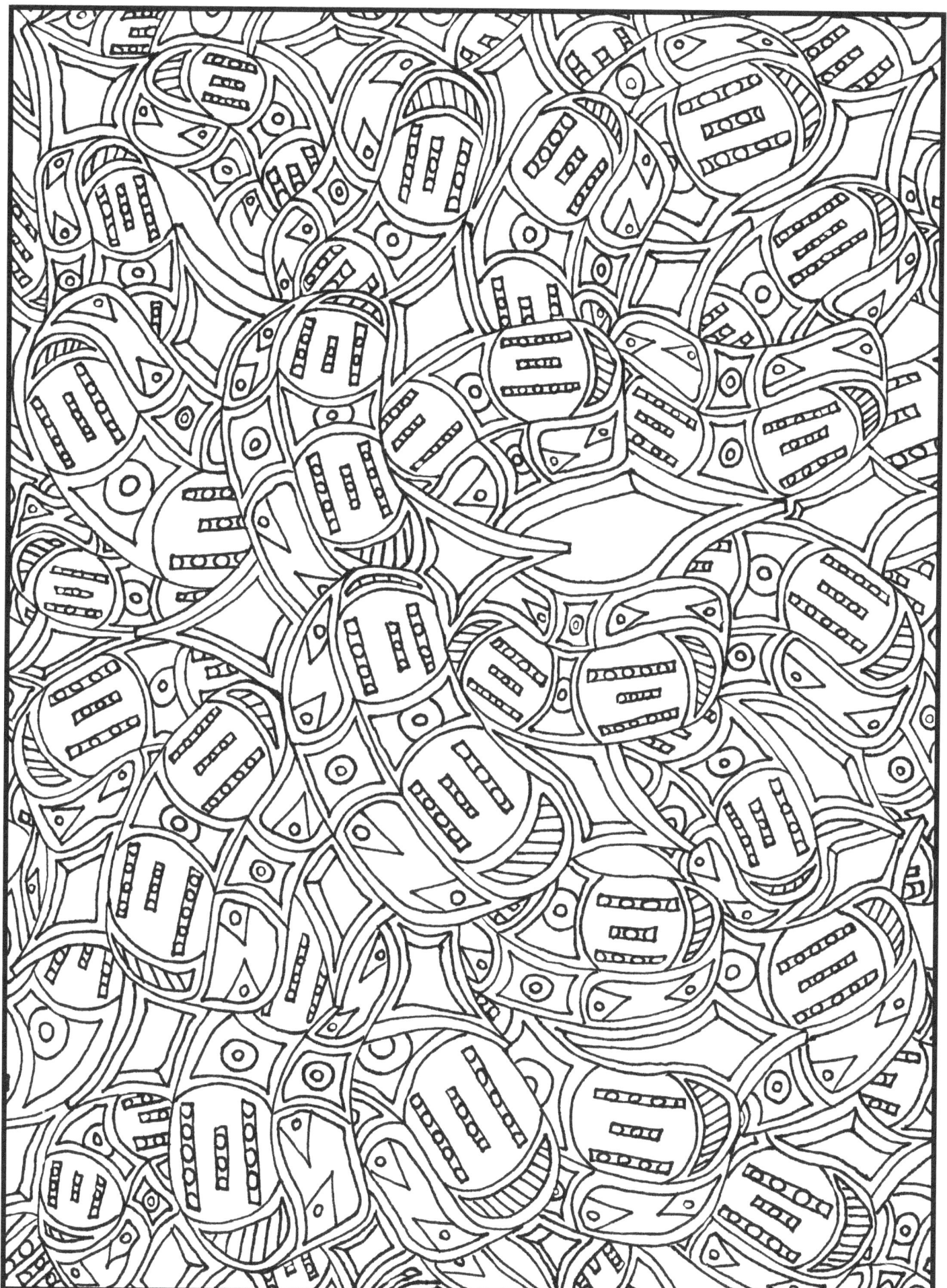

© Damone Heins

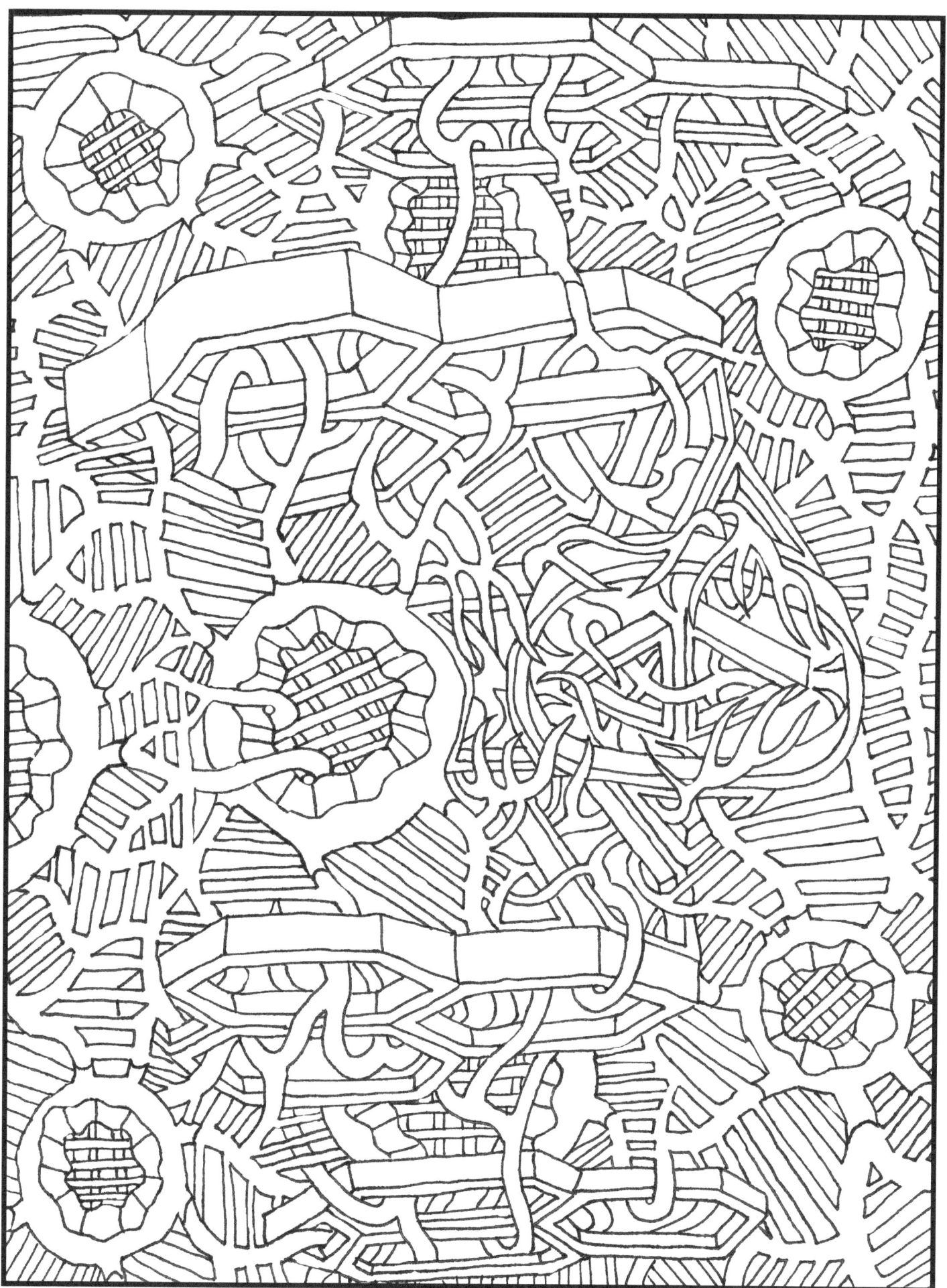

© Damone Heins

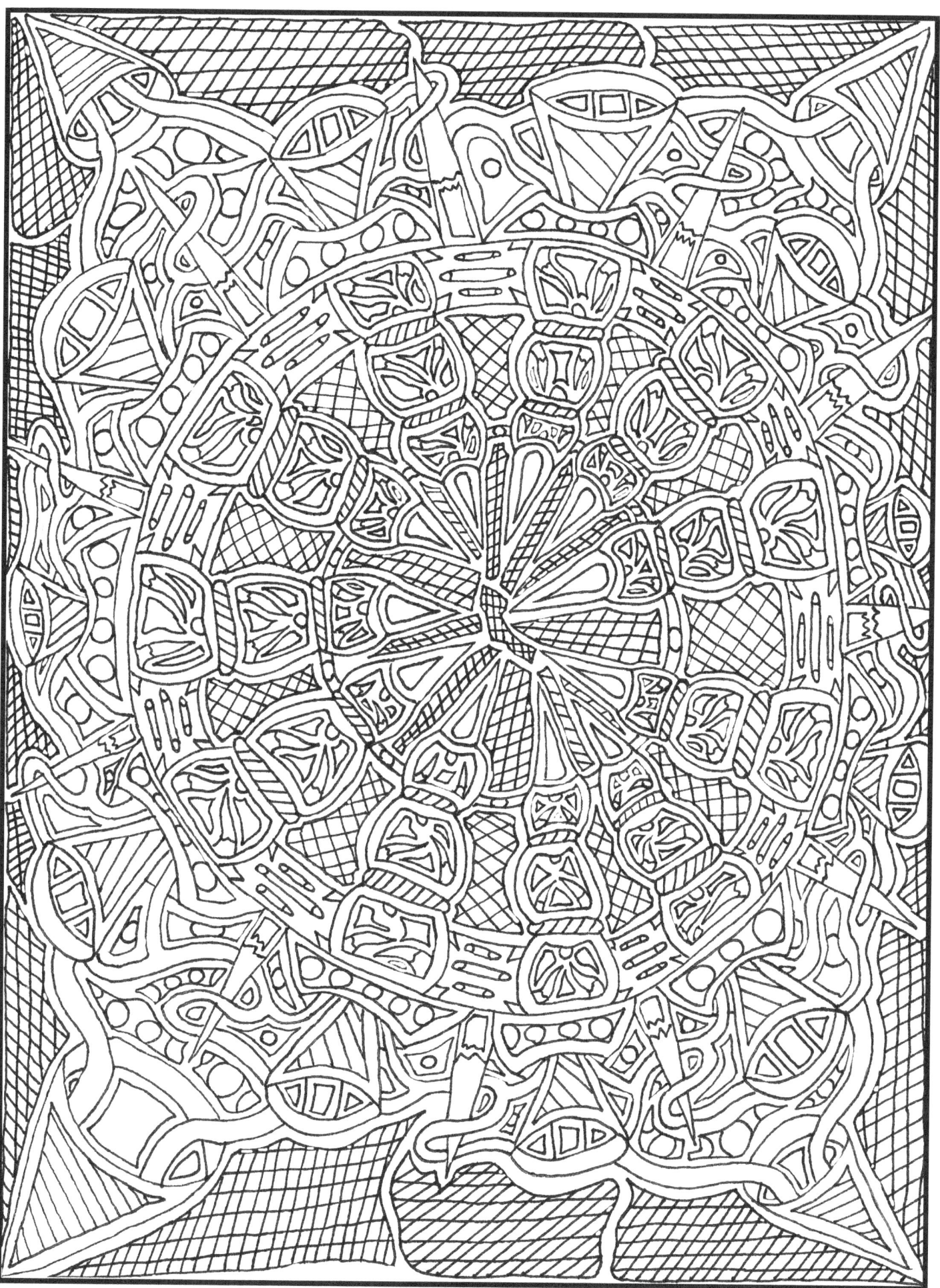

© Damone Heins

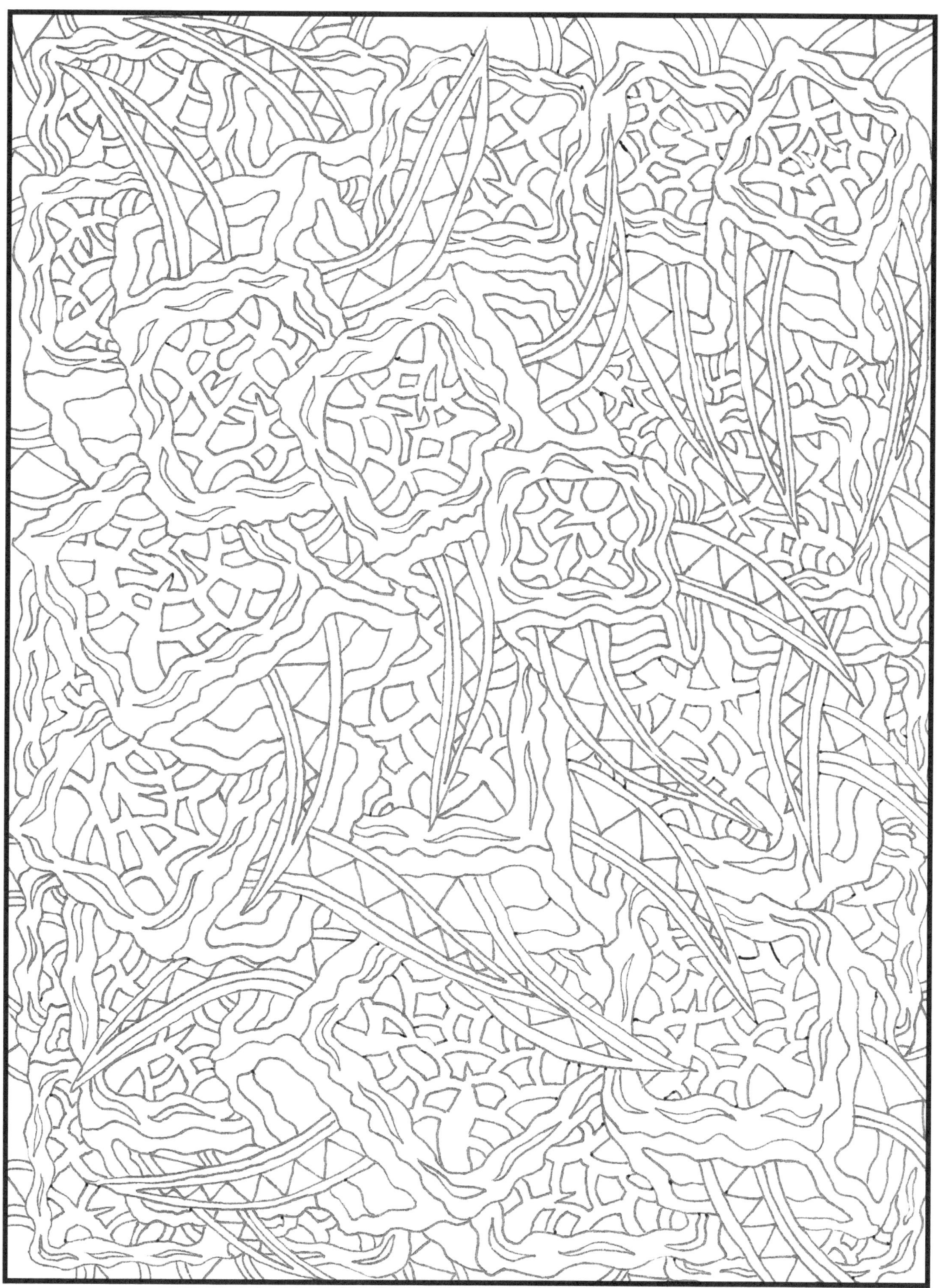

© Damone Heins

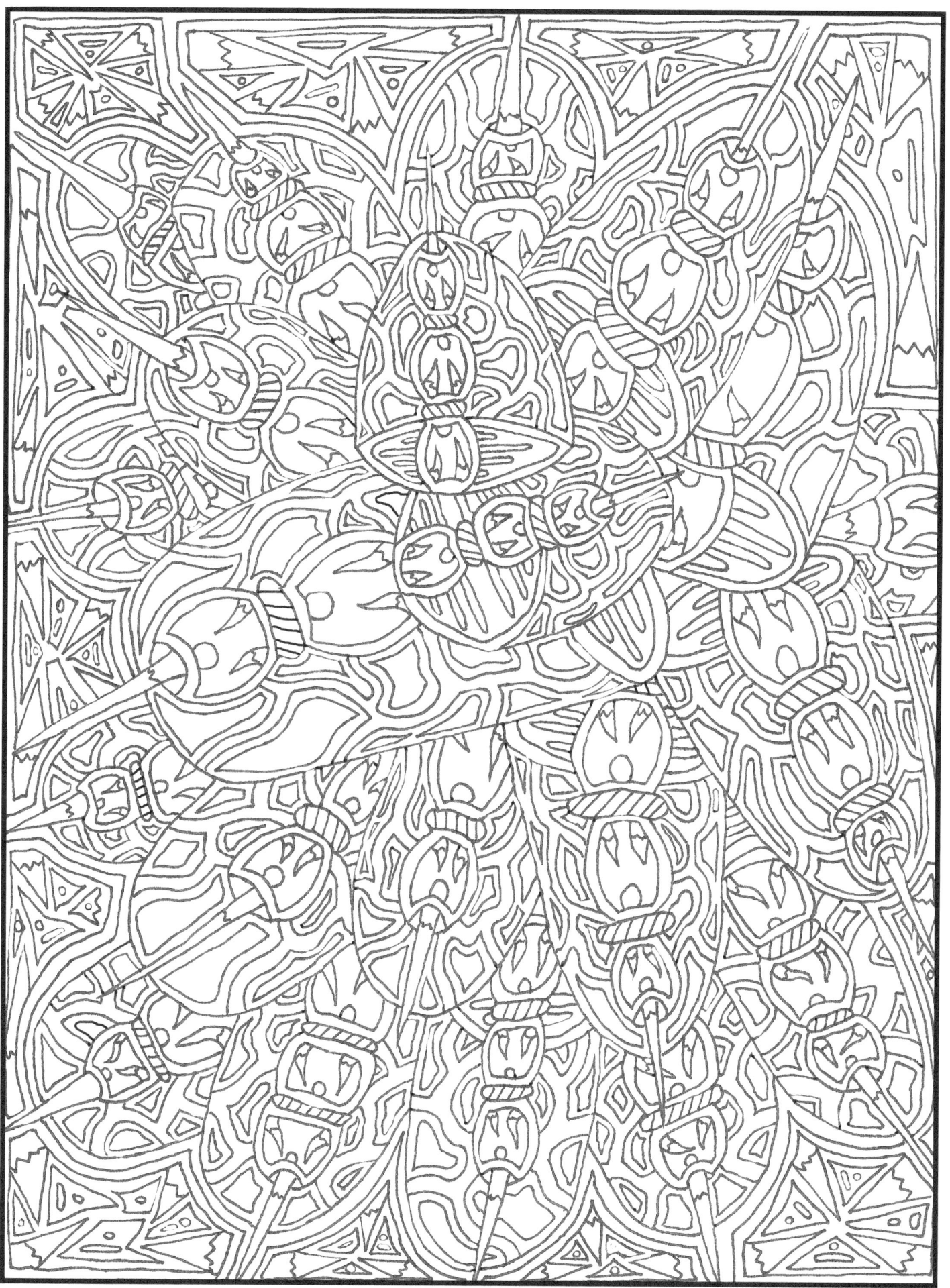

© Damone Heins

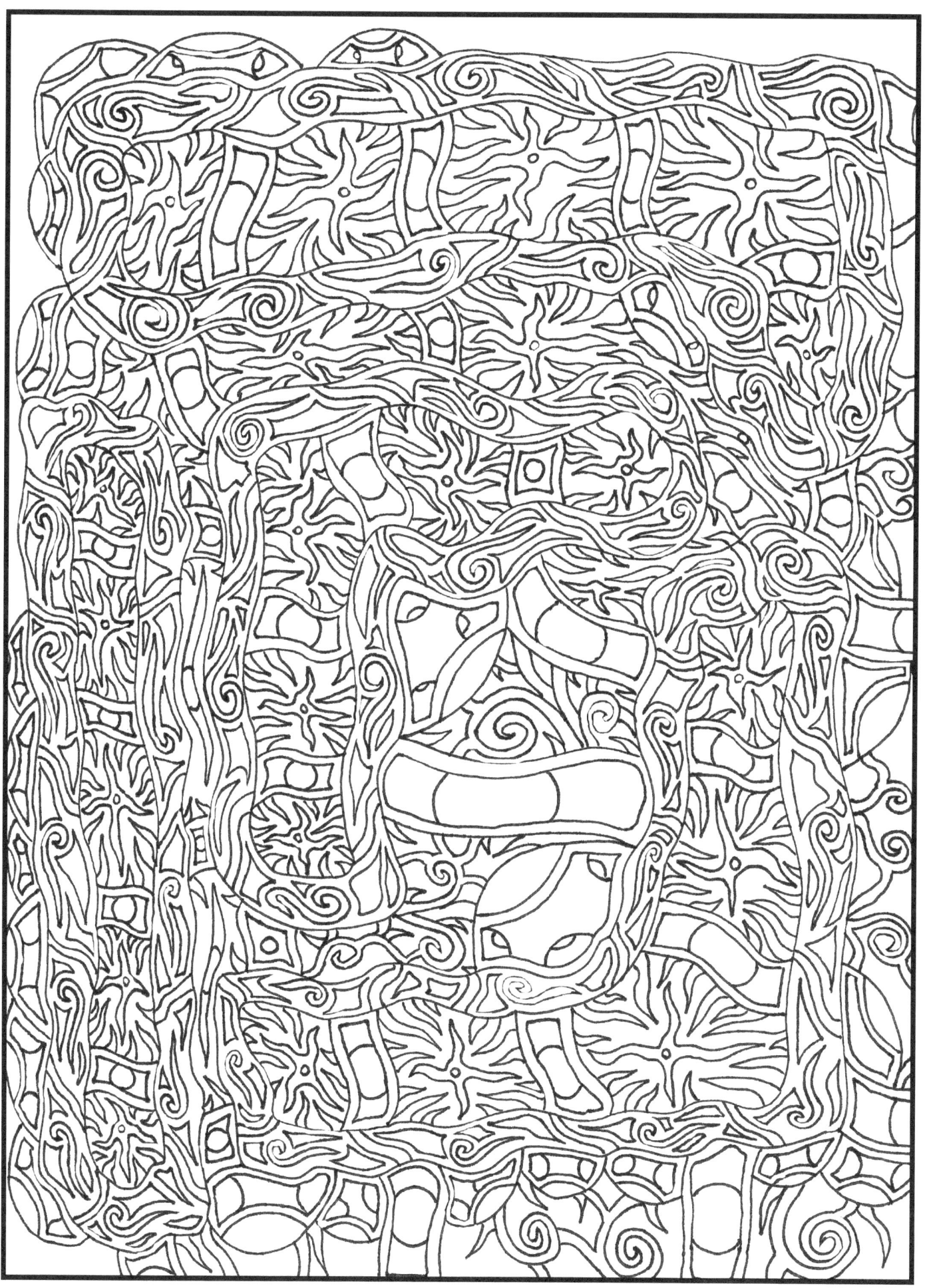

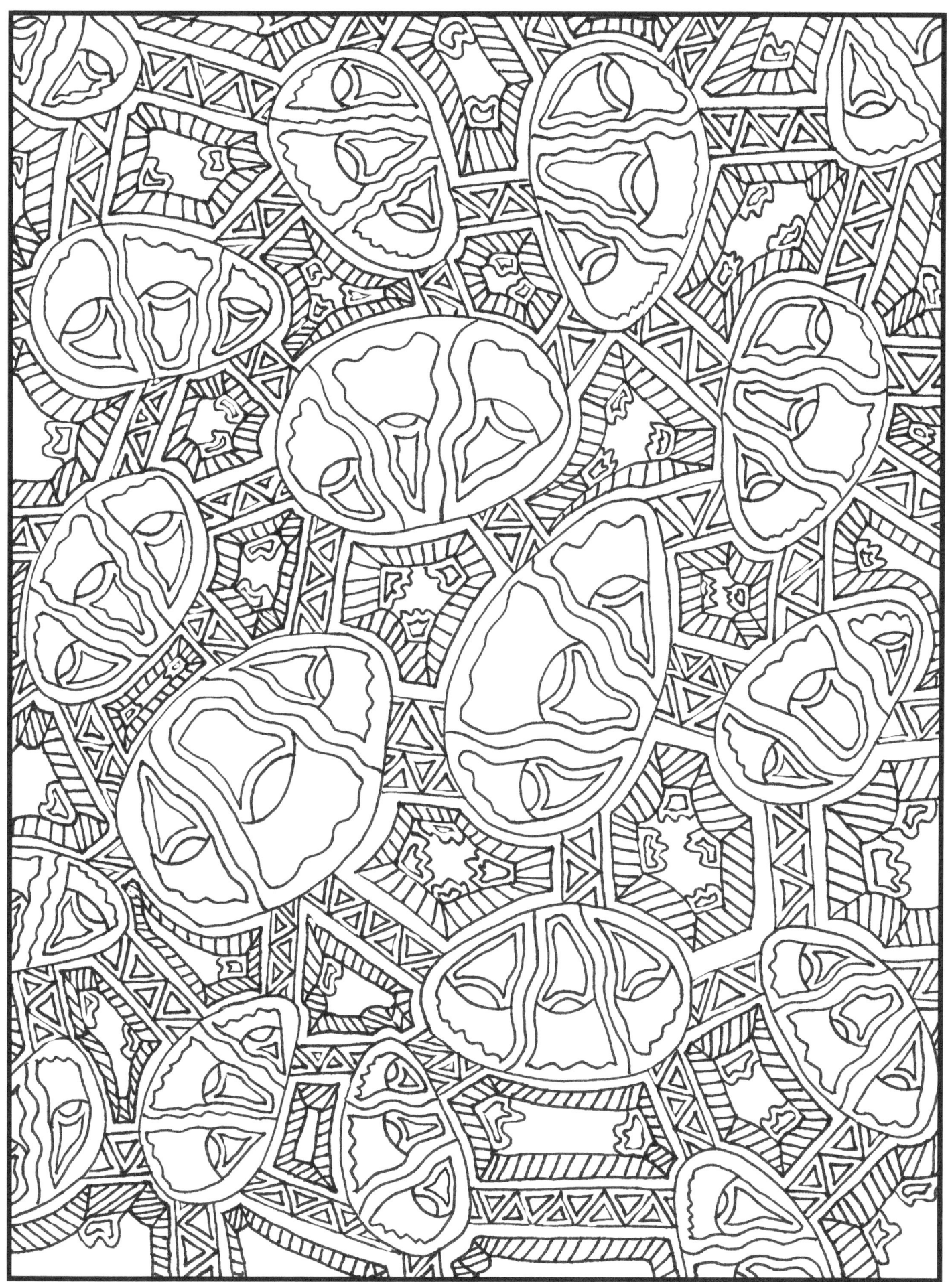

© Damone Heins

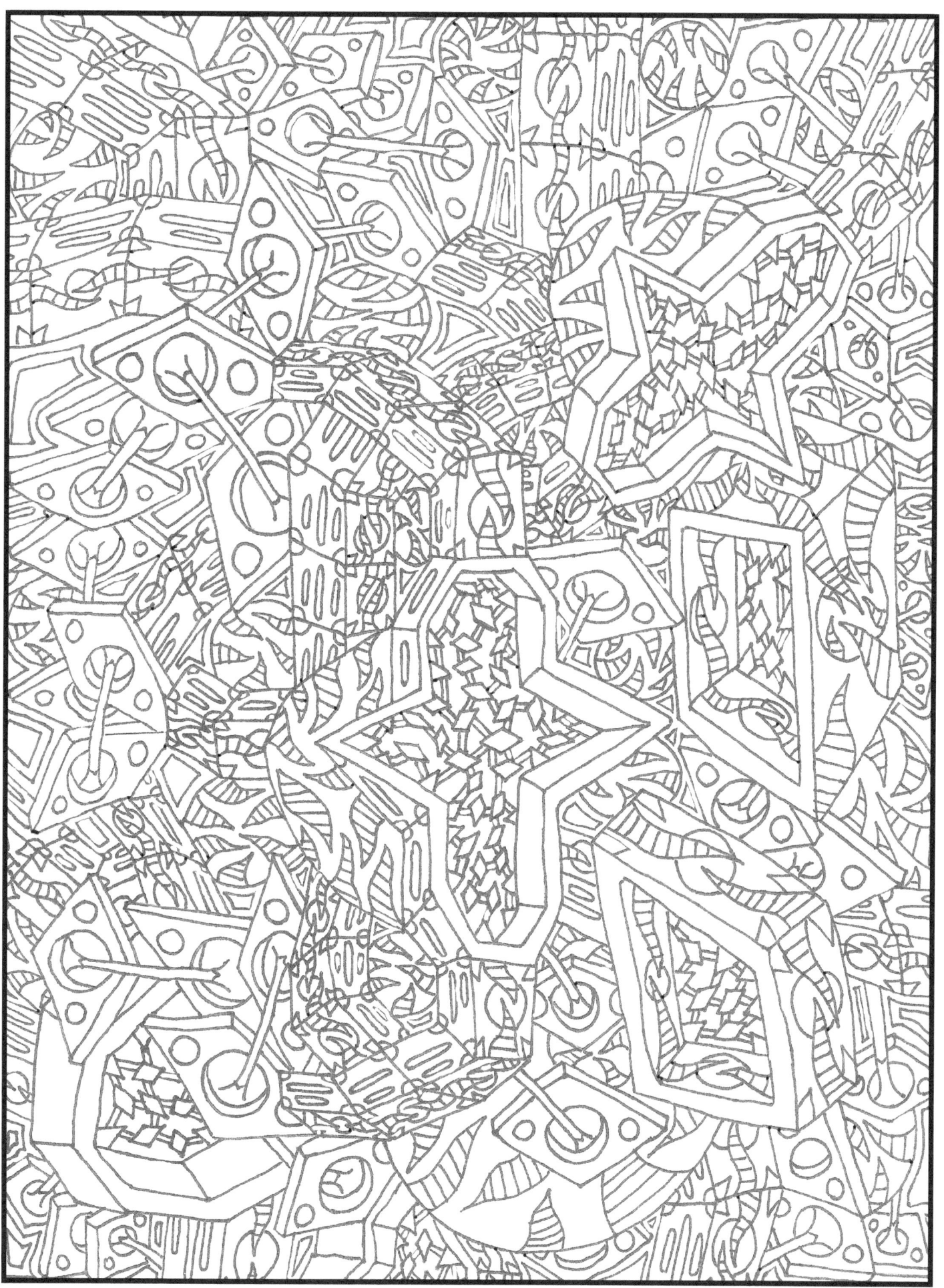

© Damone Heins

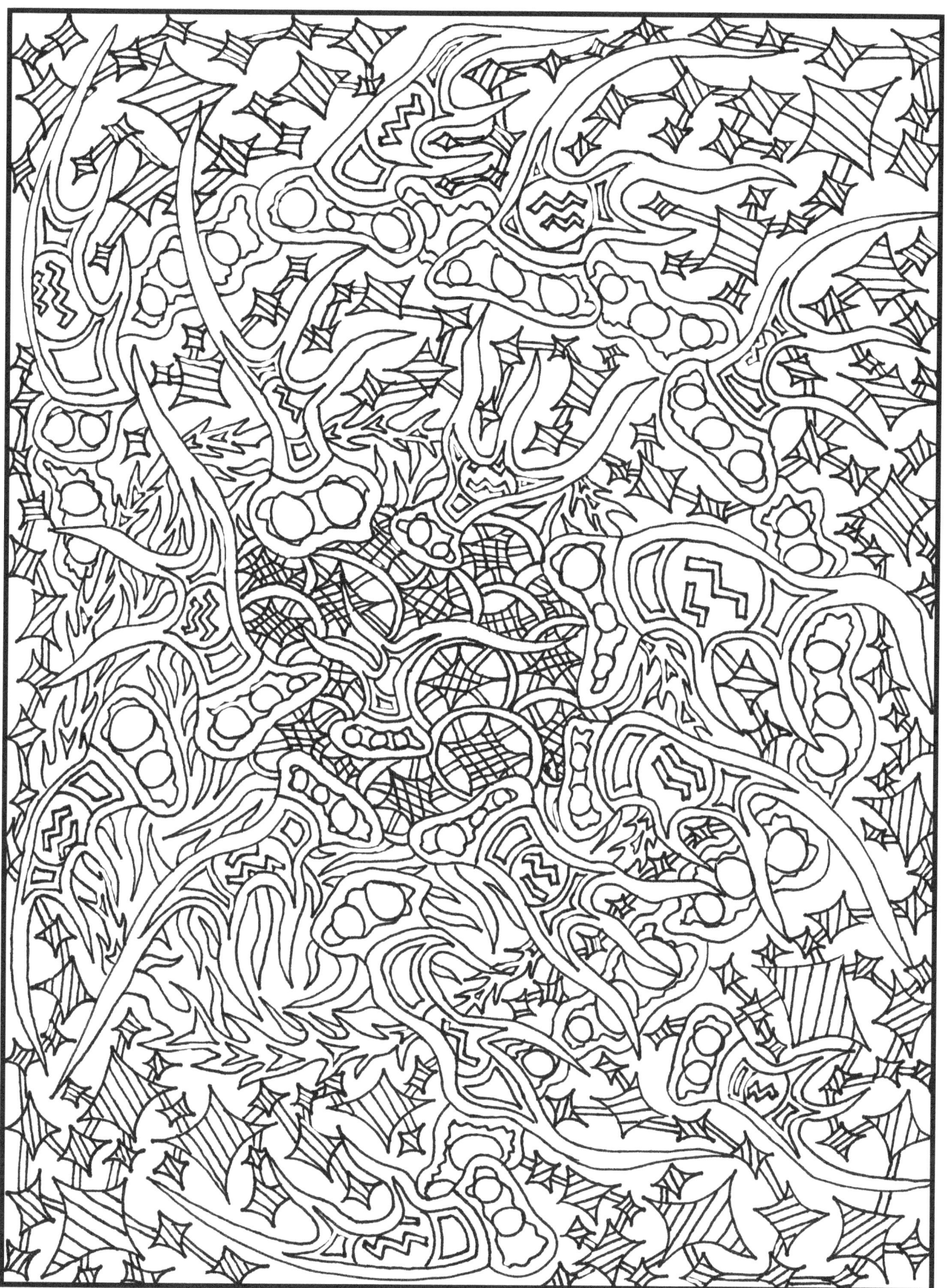

© Damone Heins

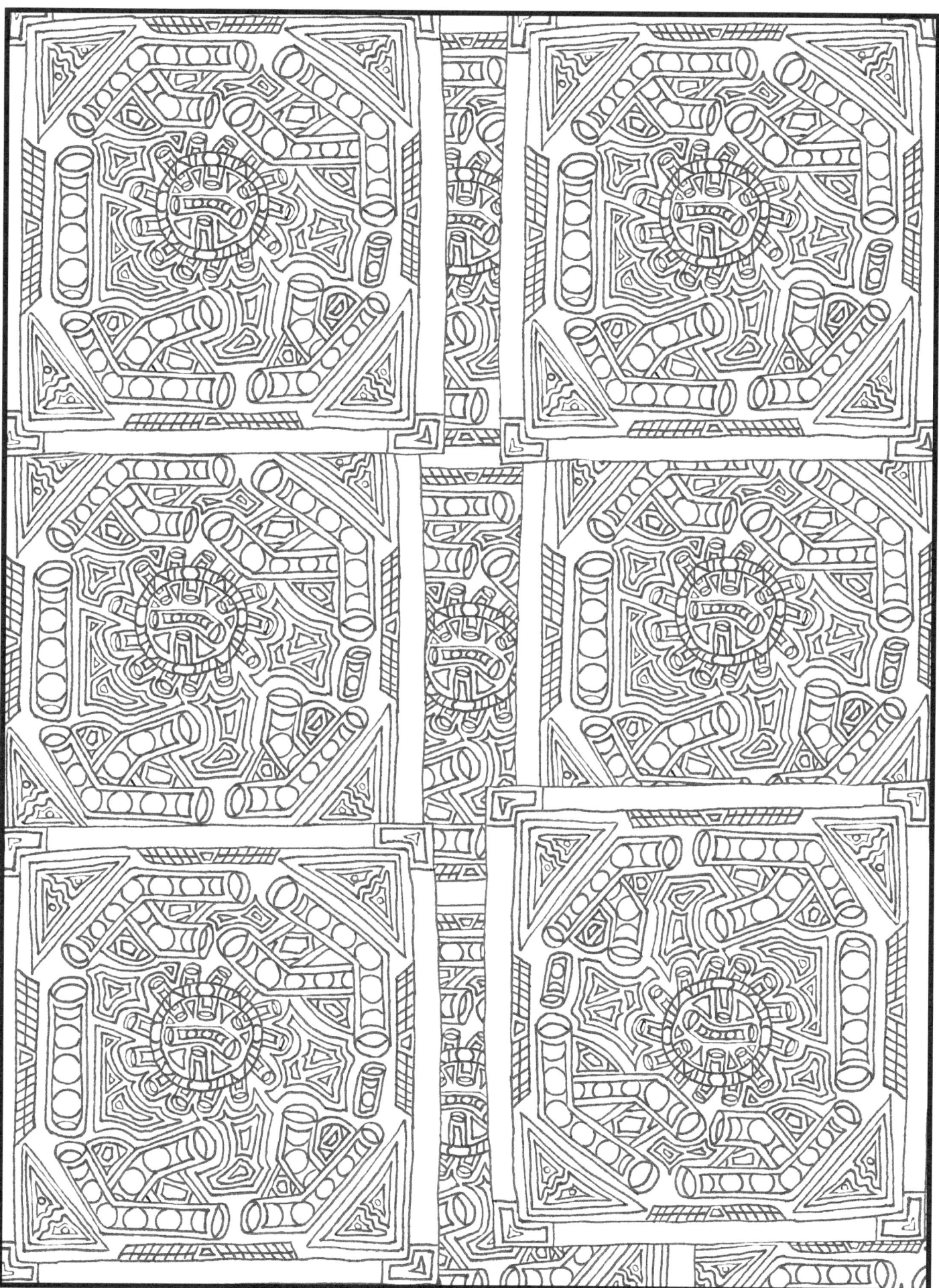

© Damone Heins

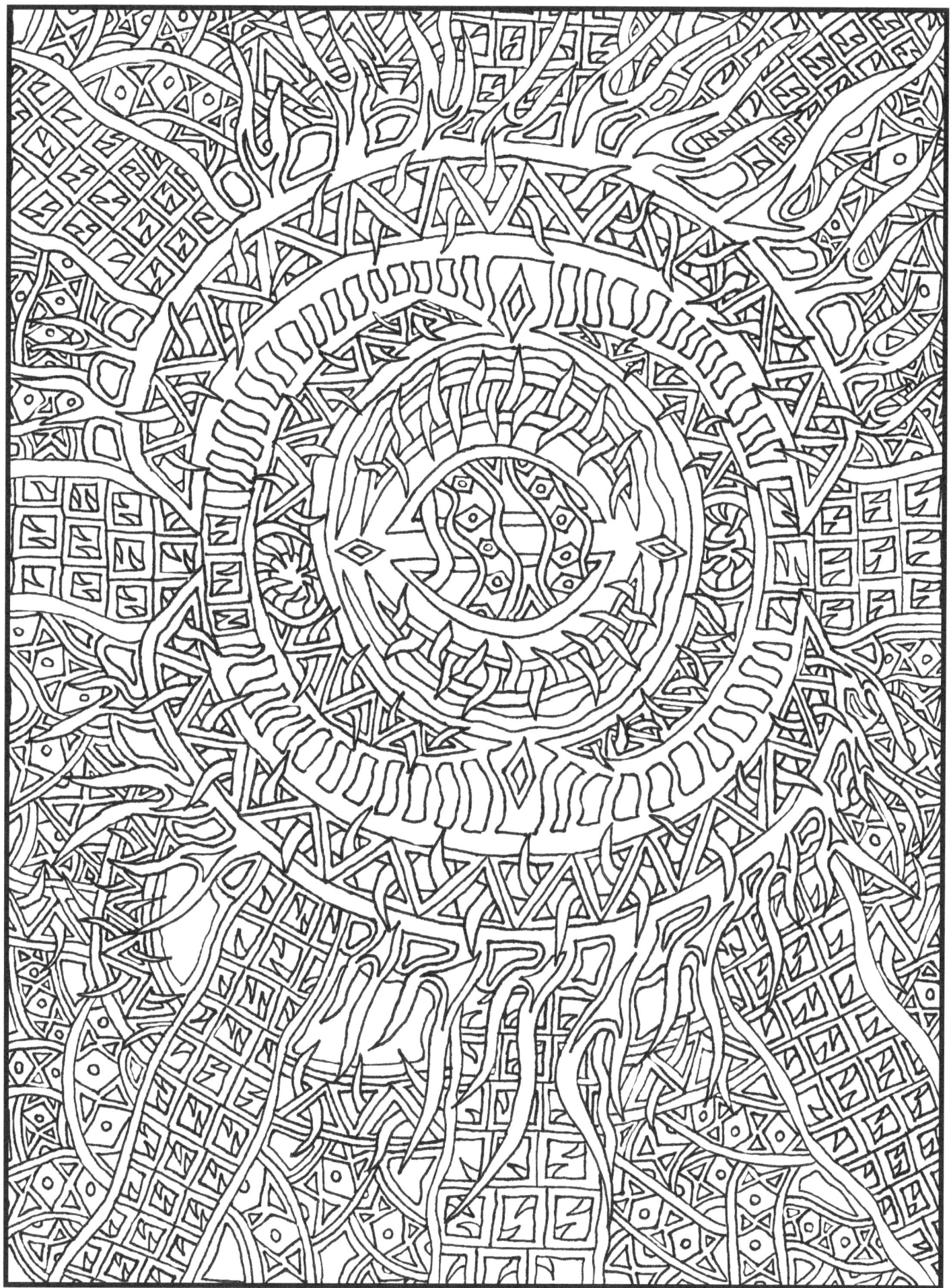

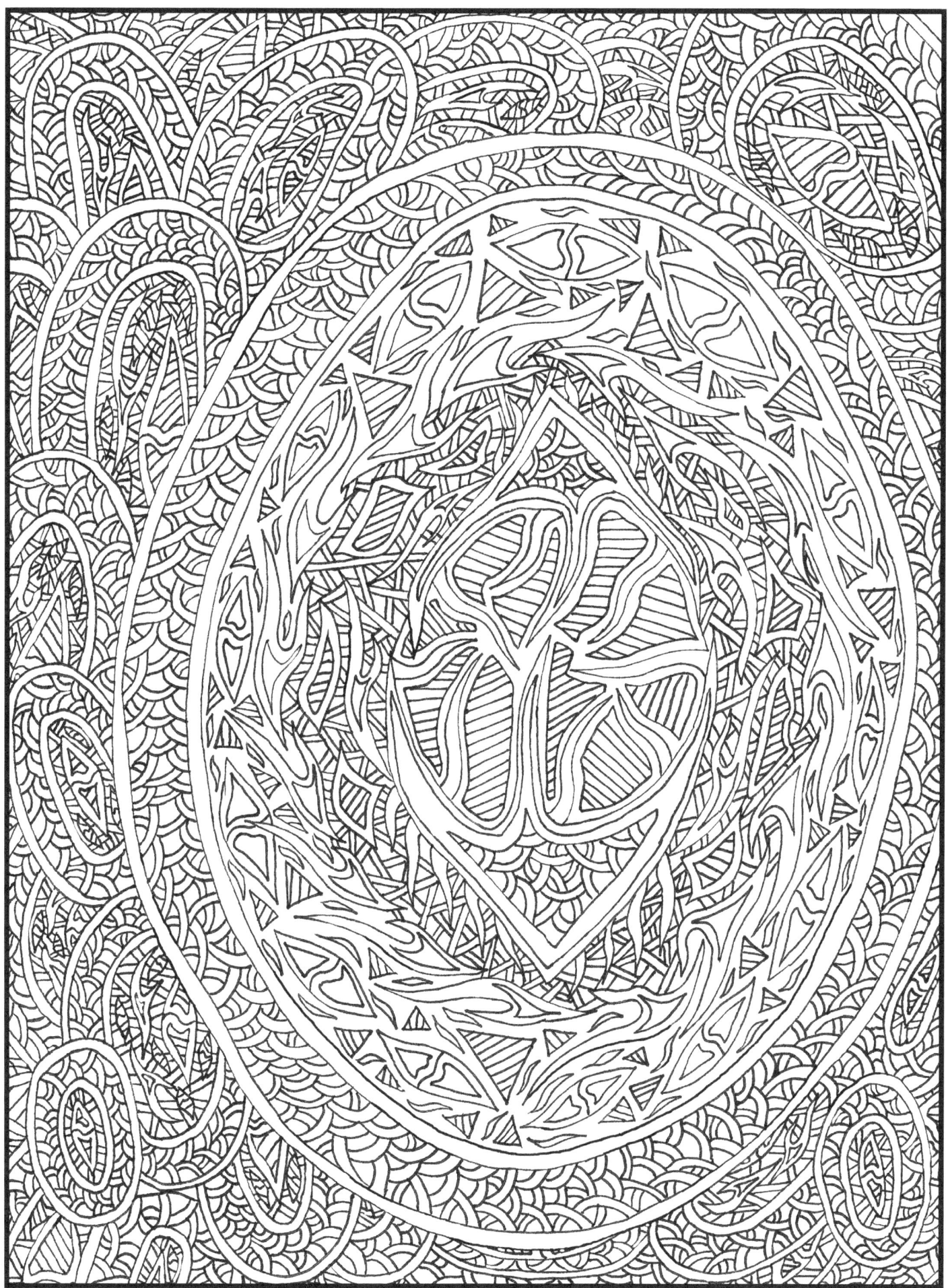

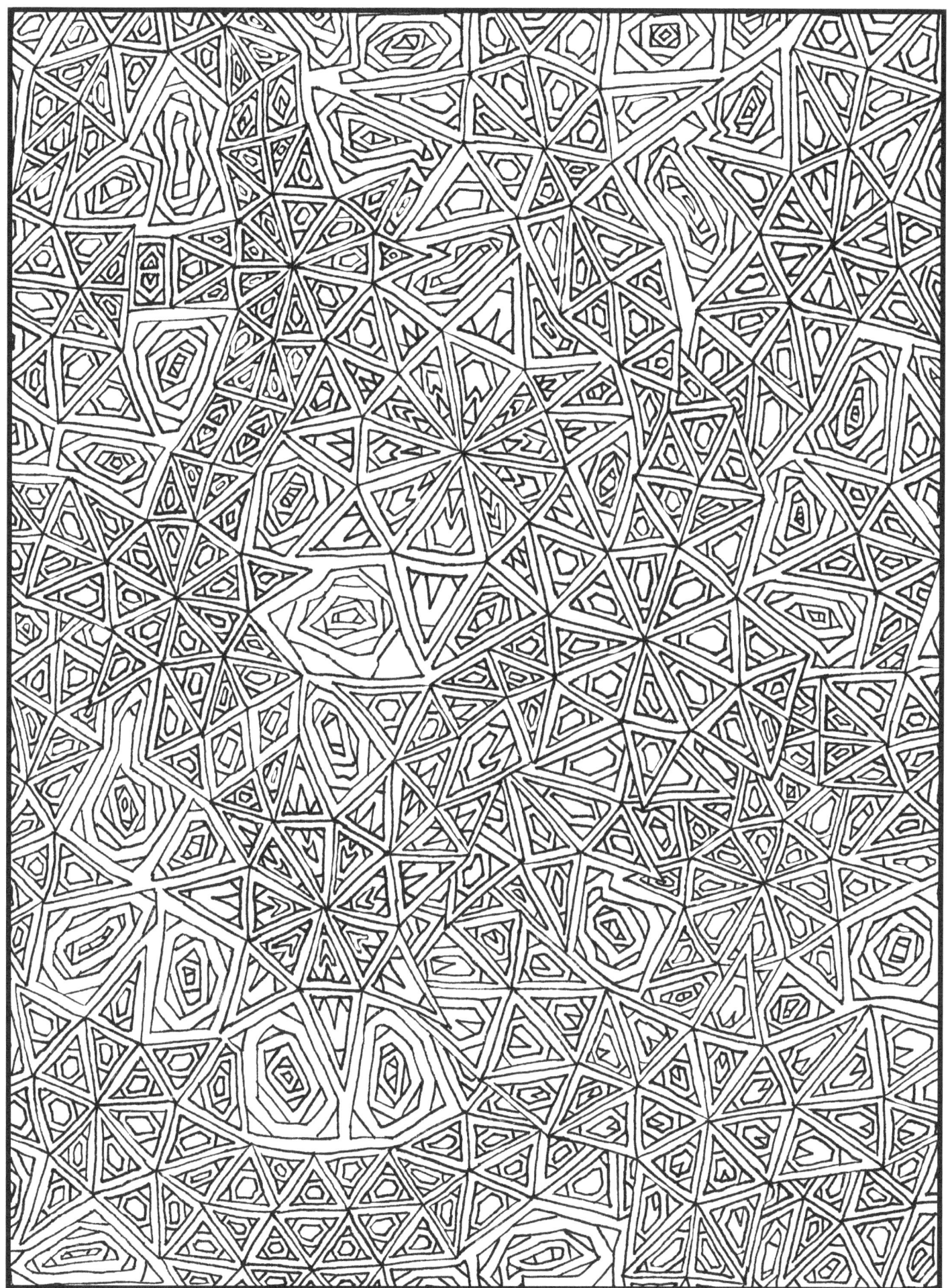

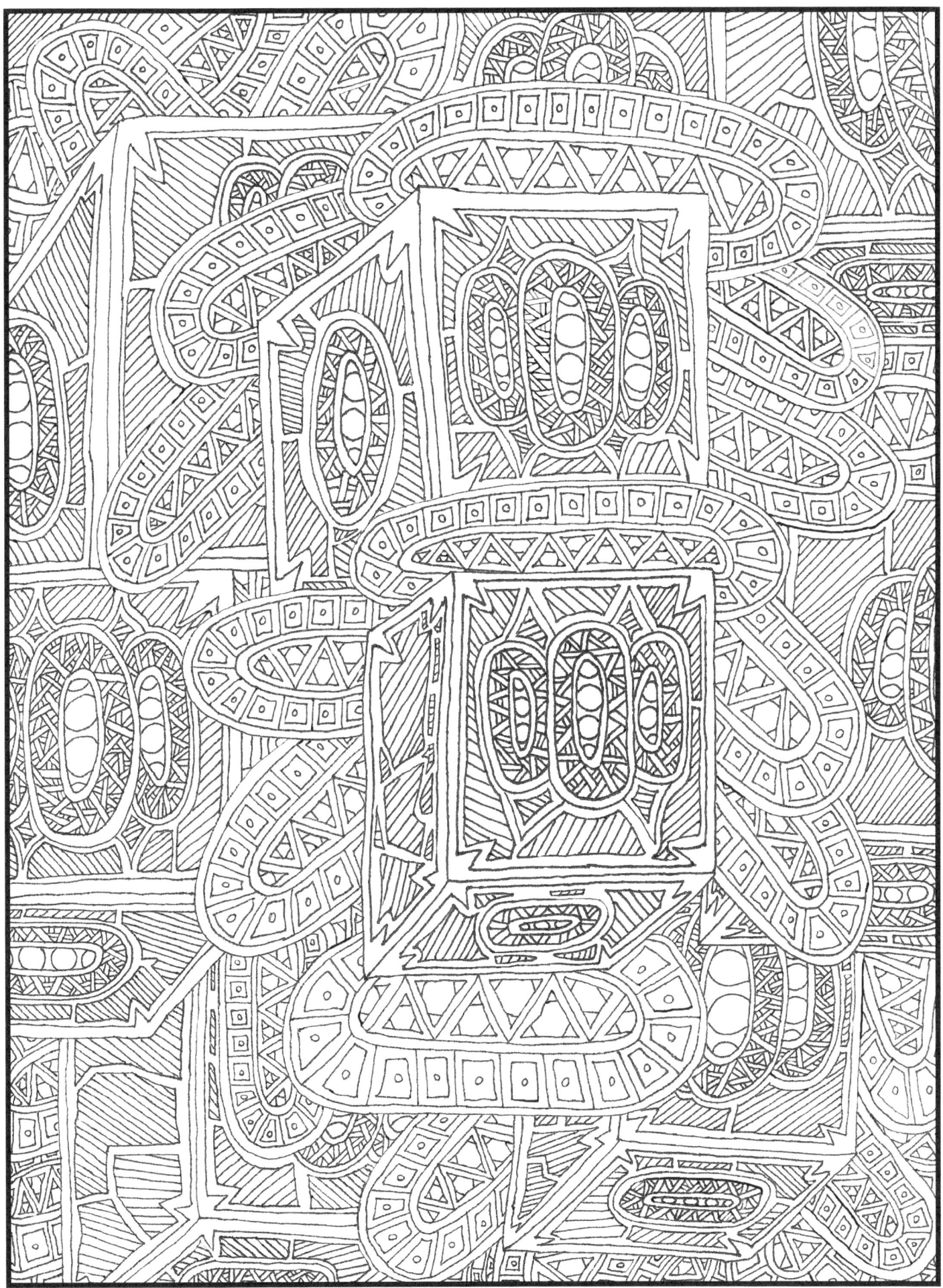

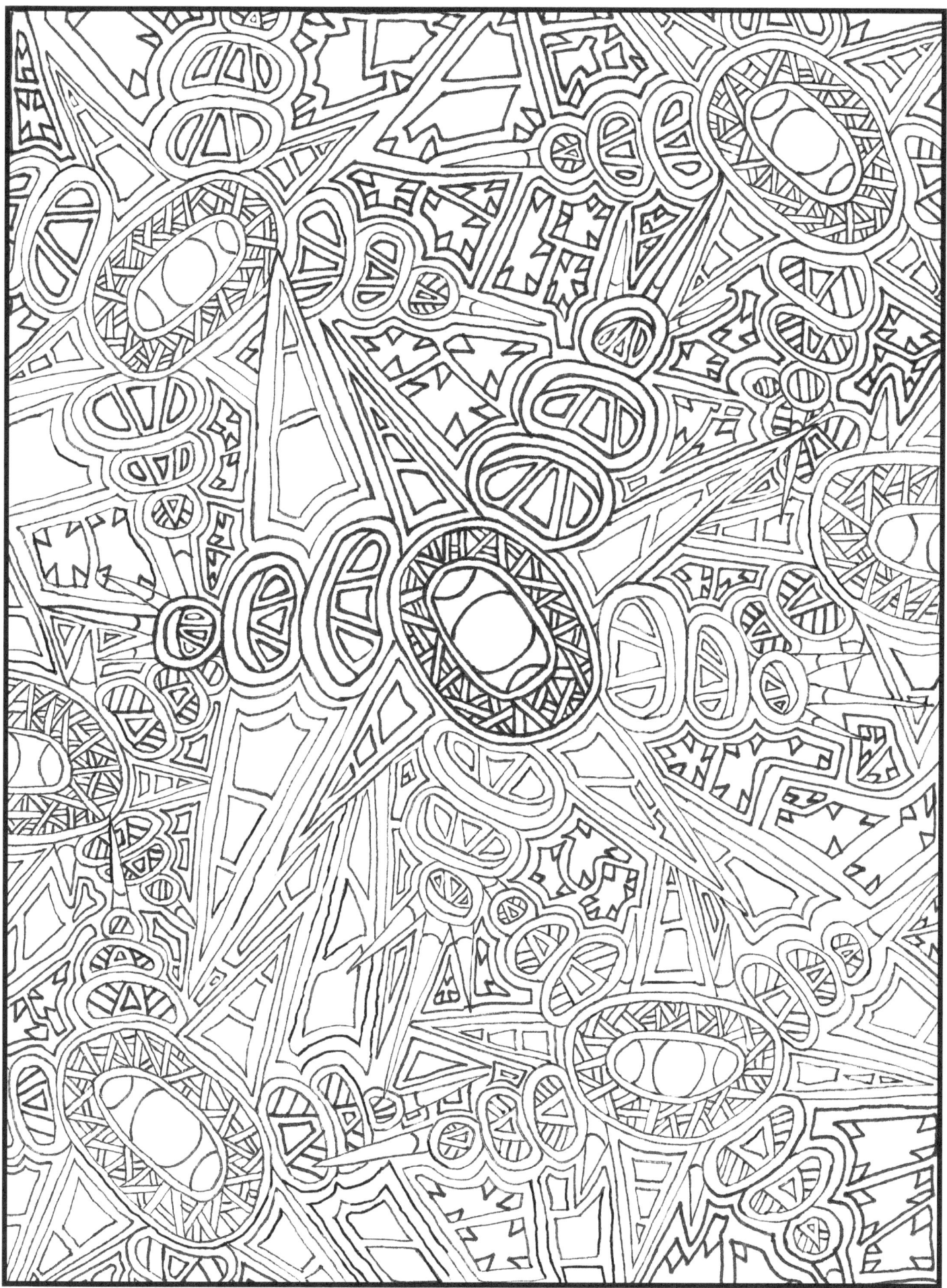

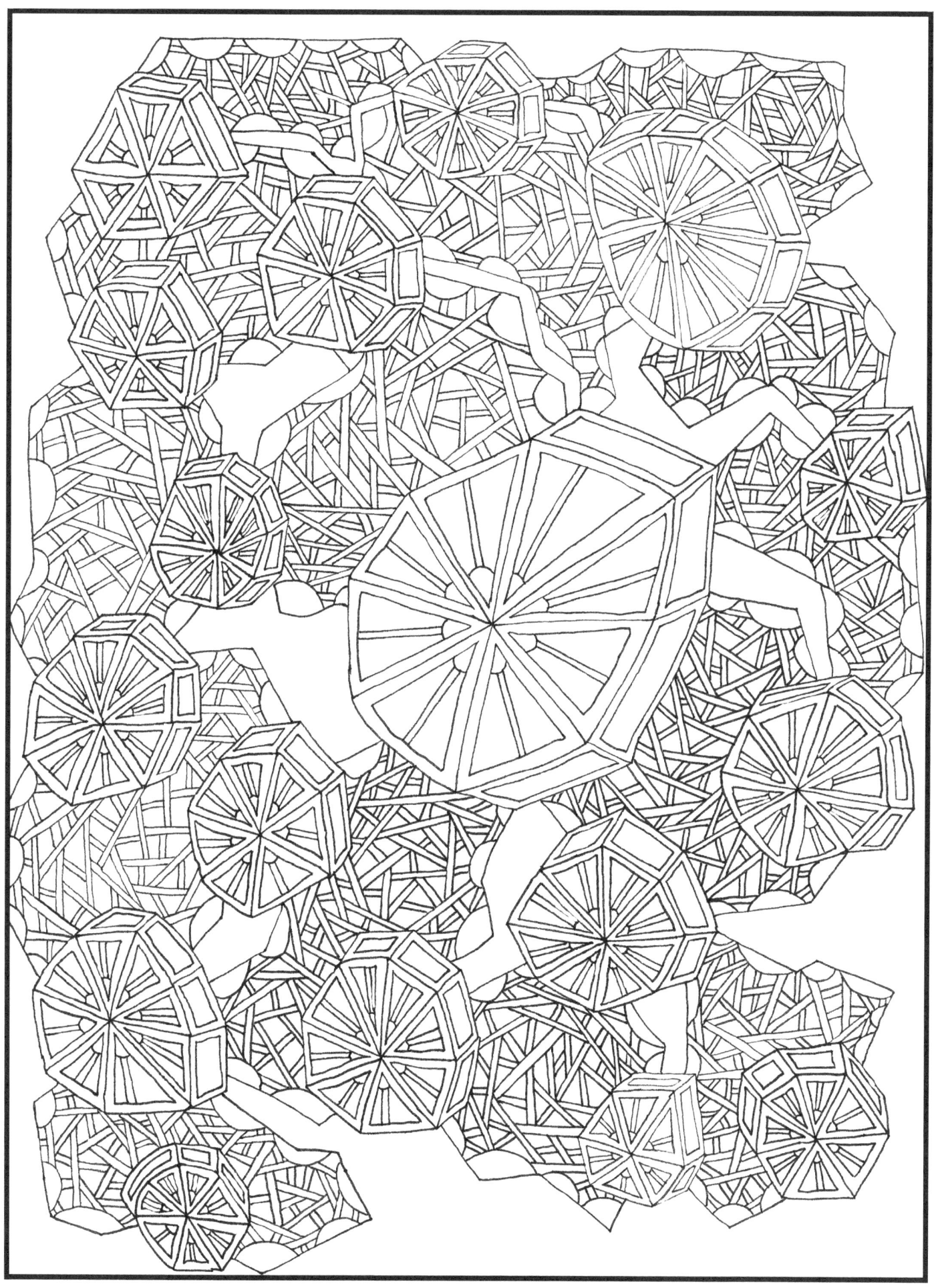

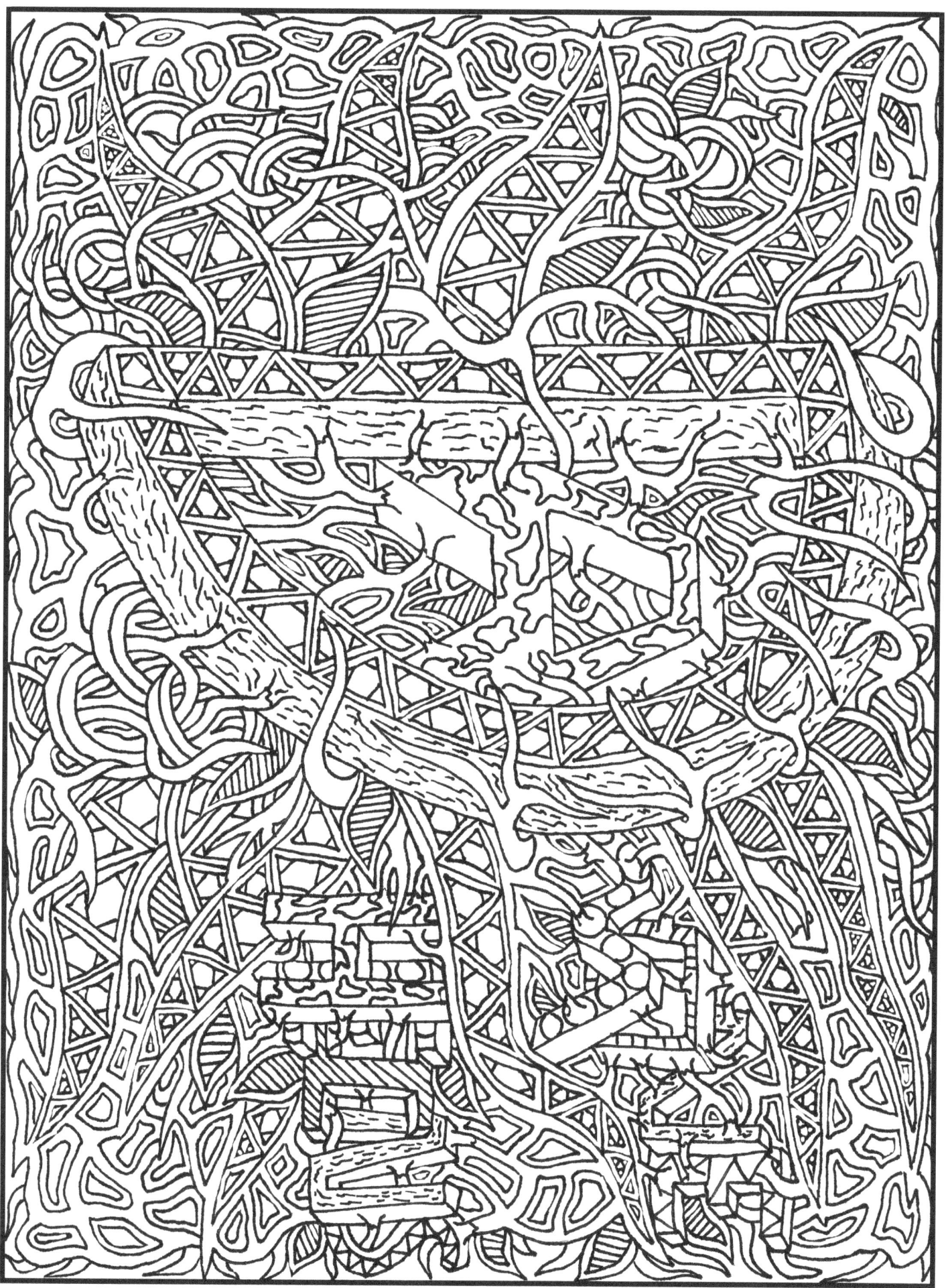

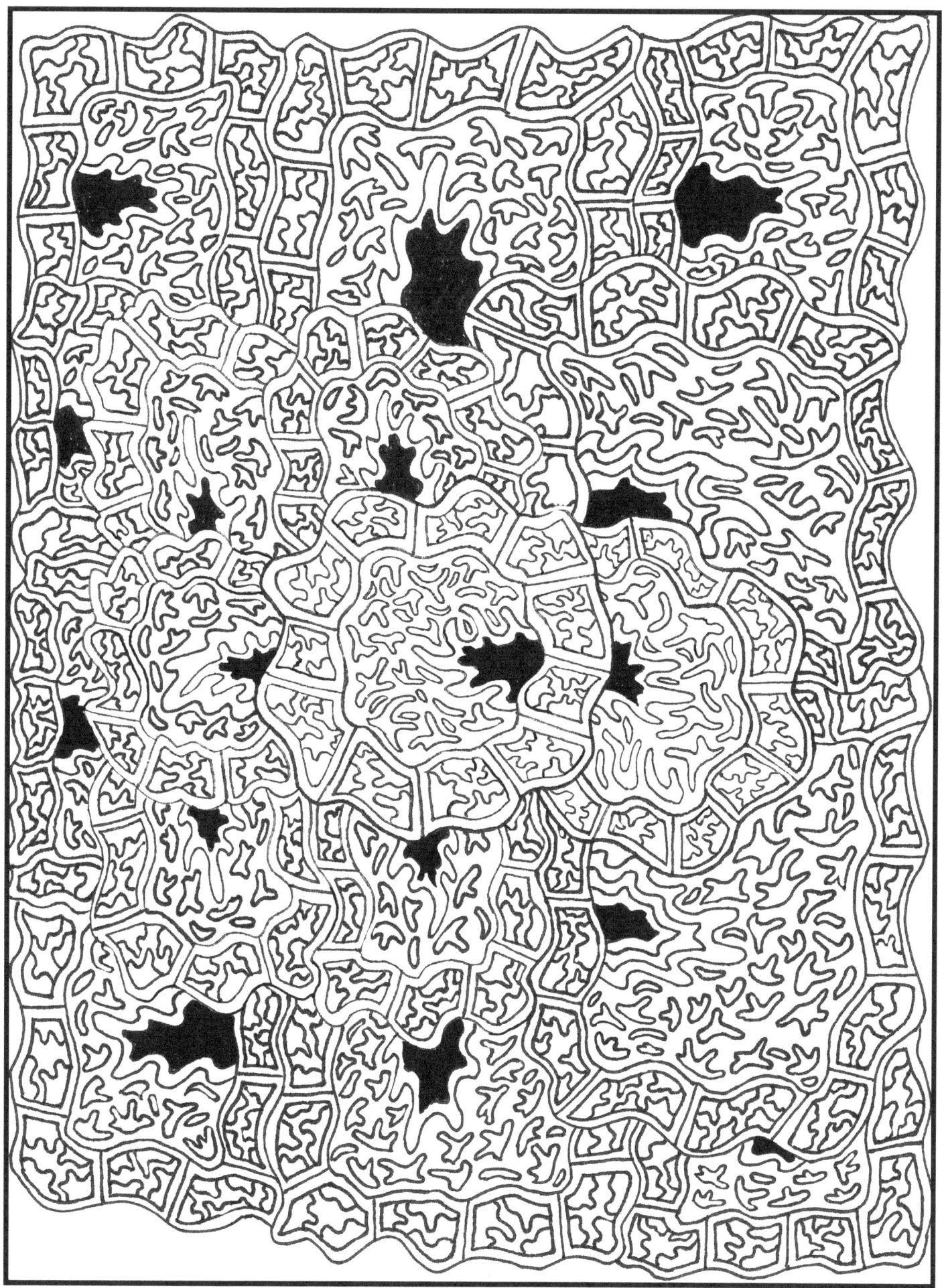

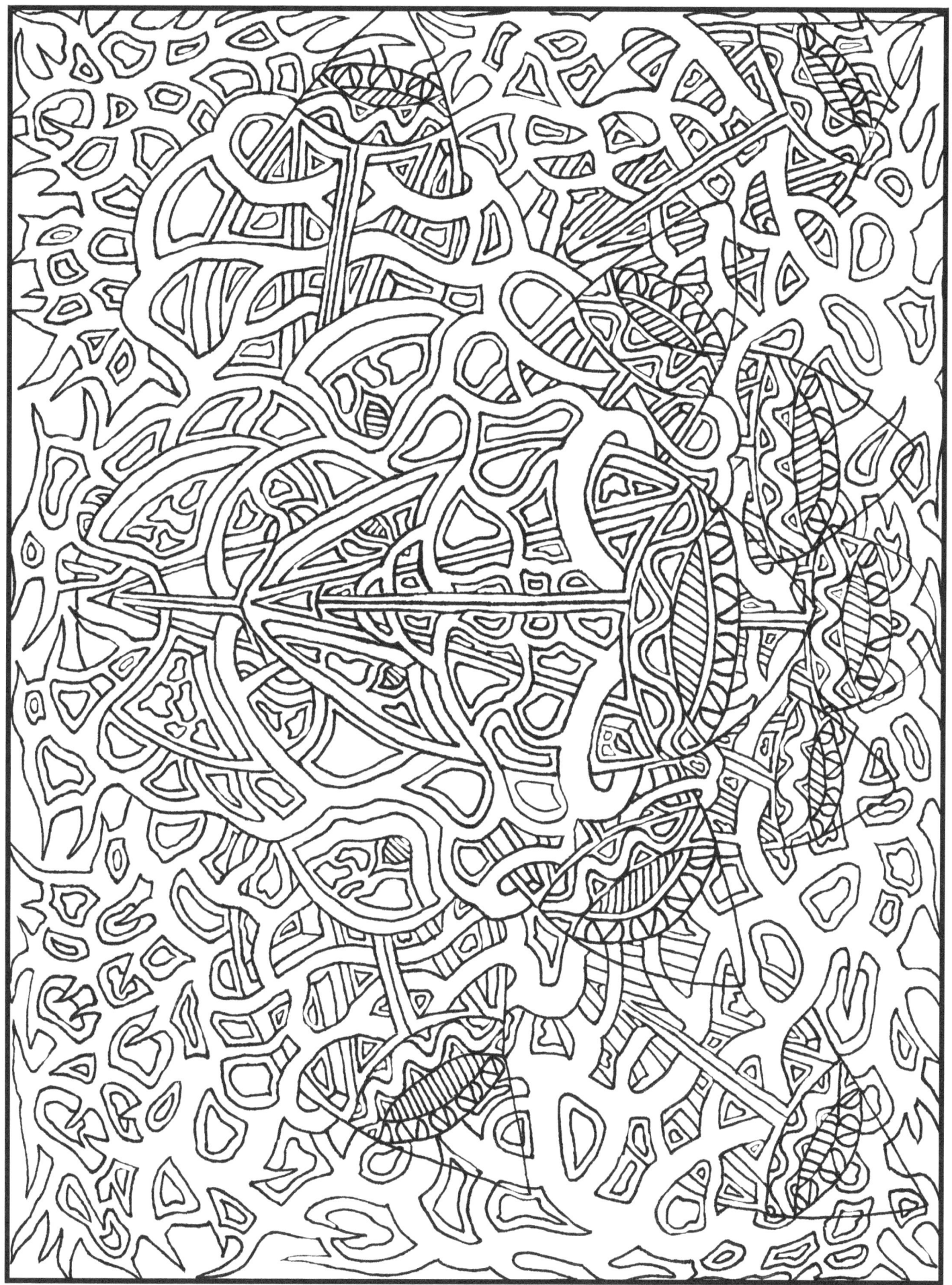

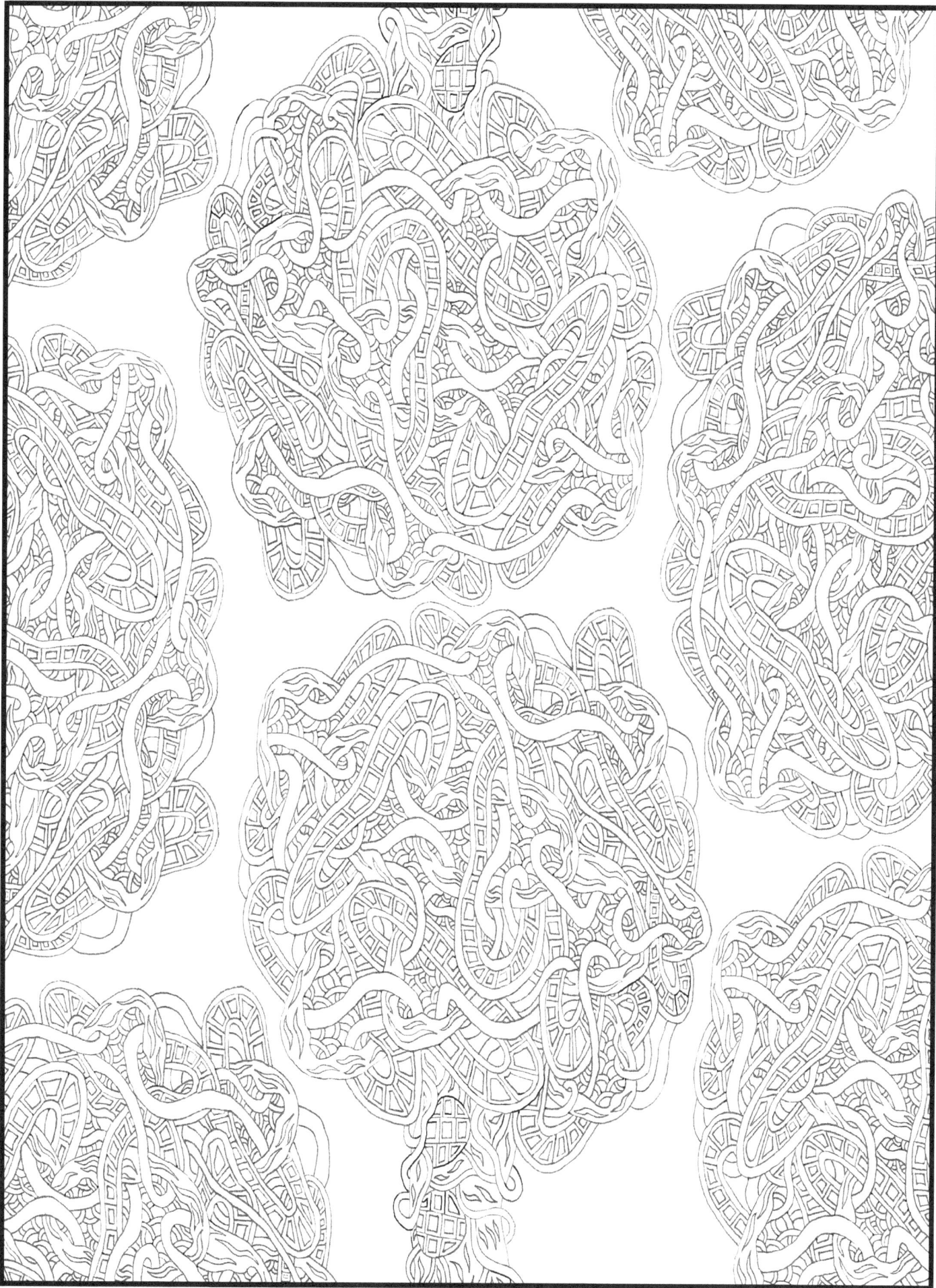

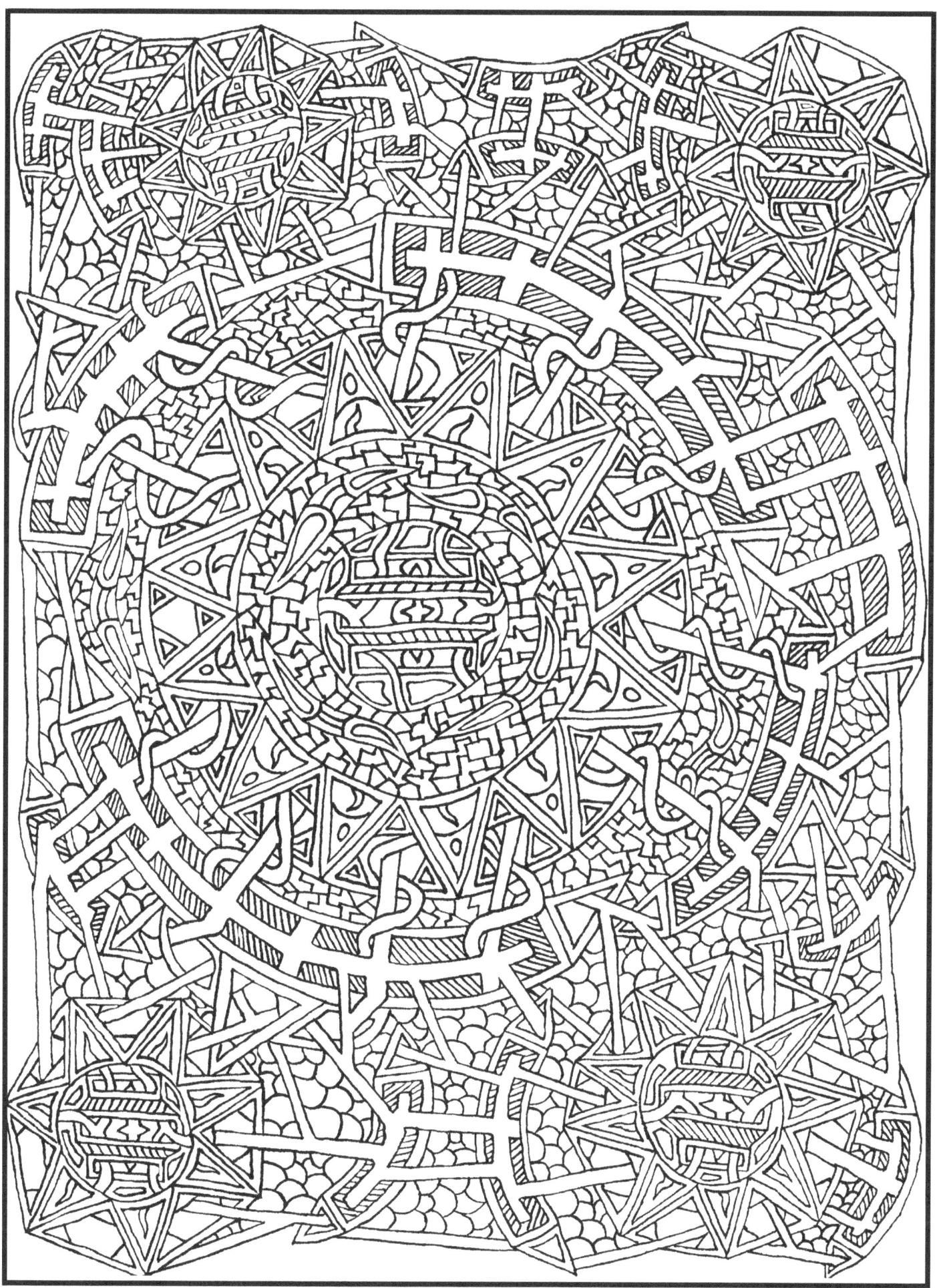

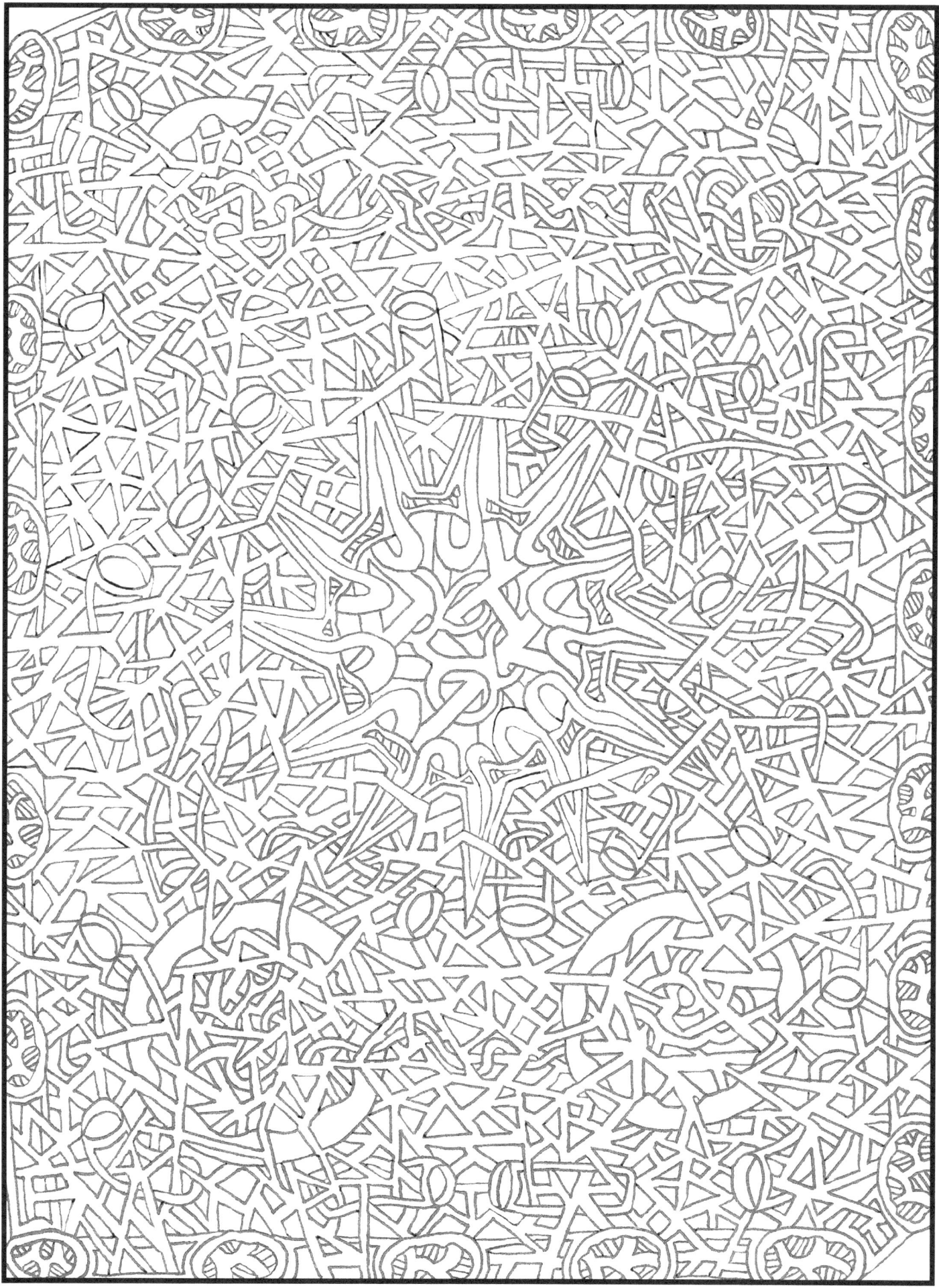

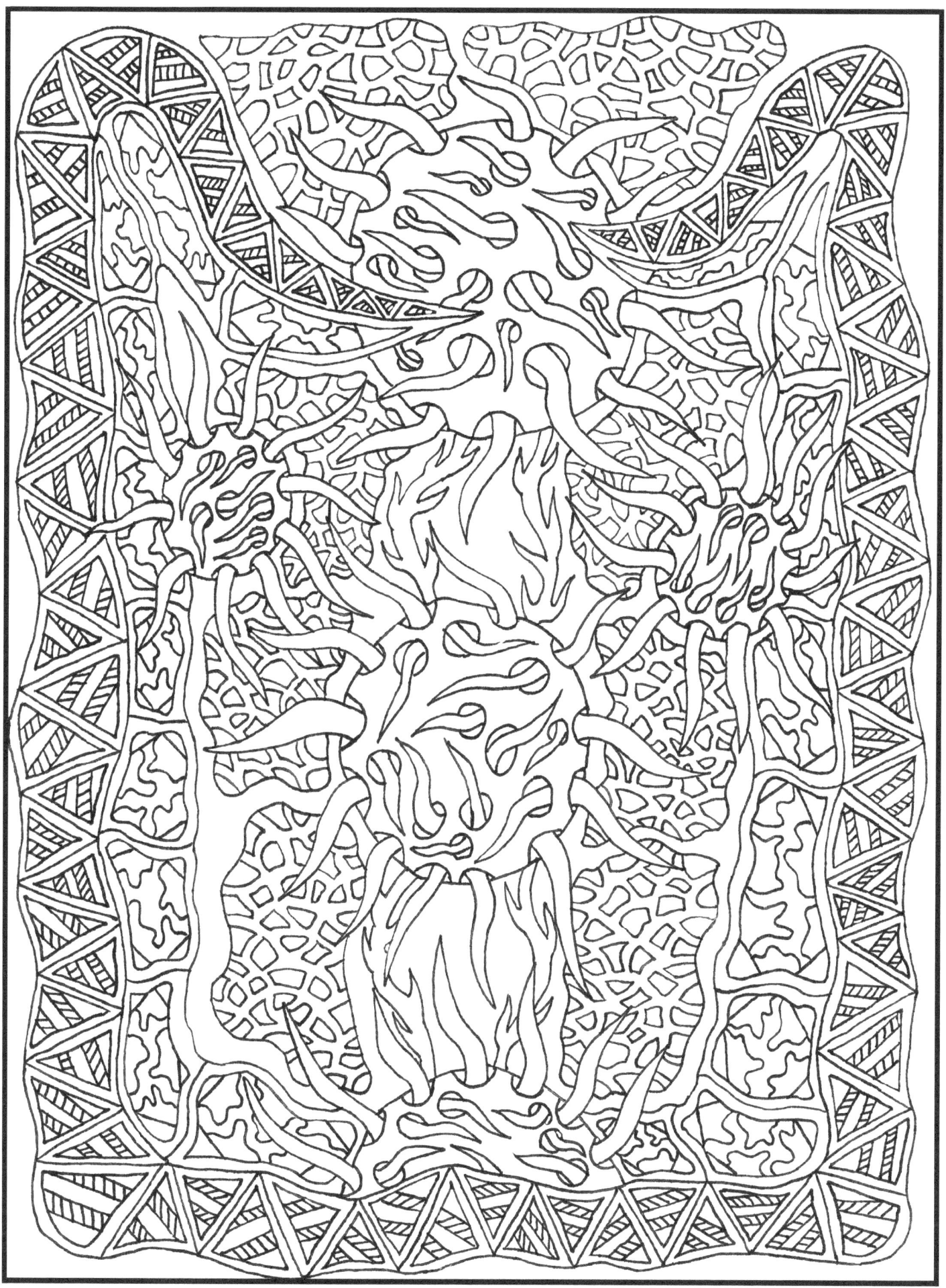

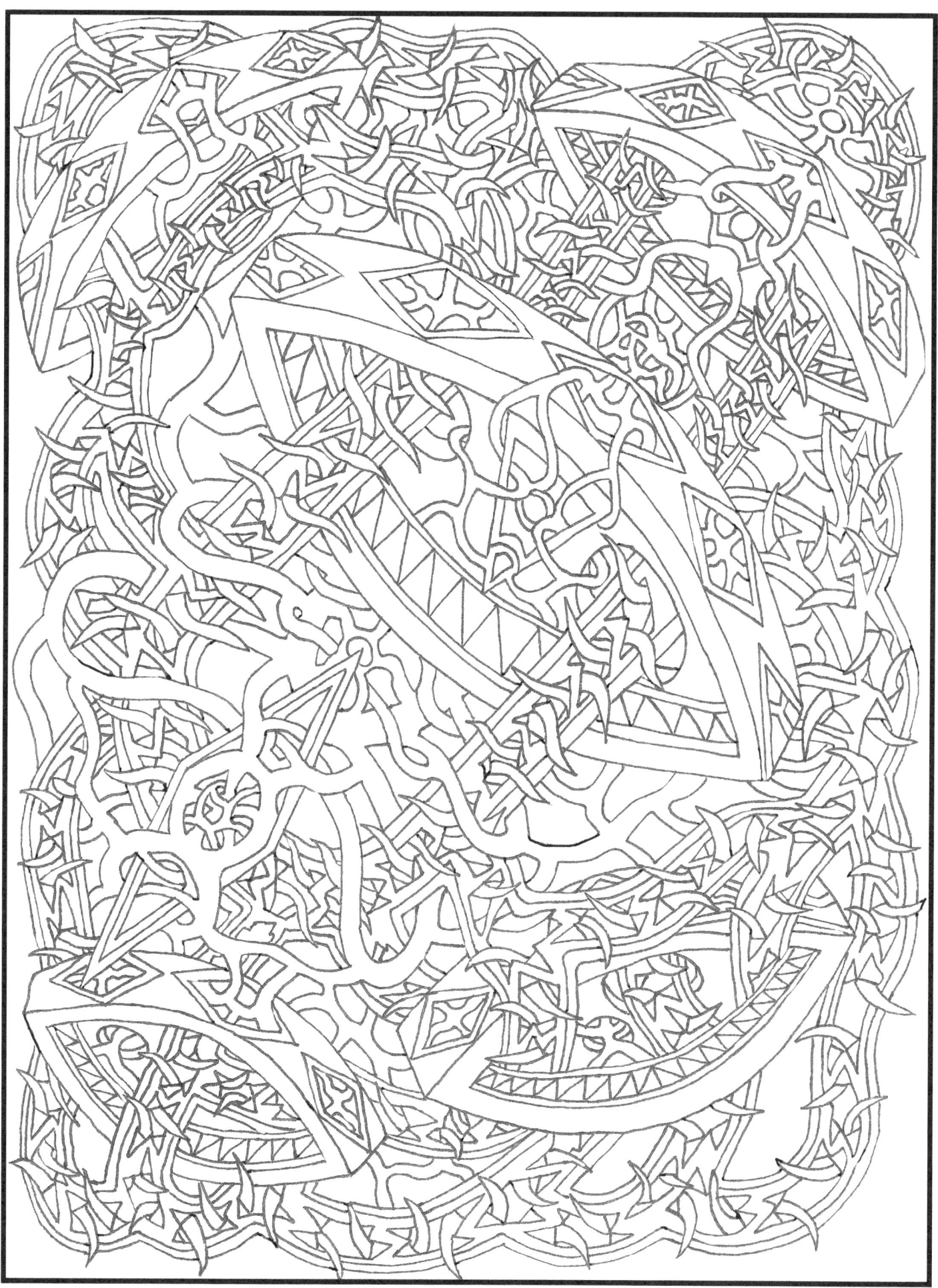

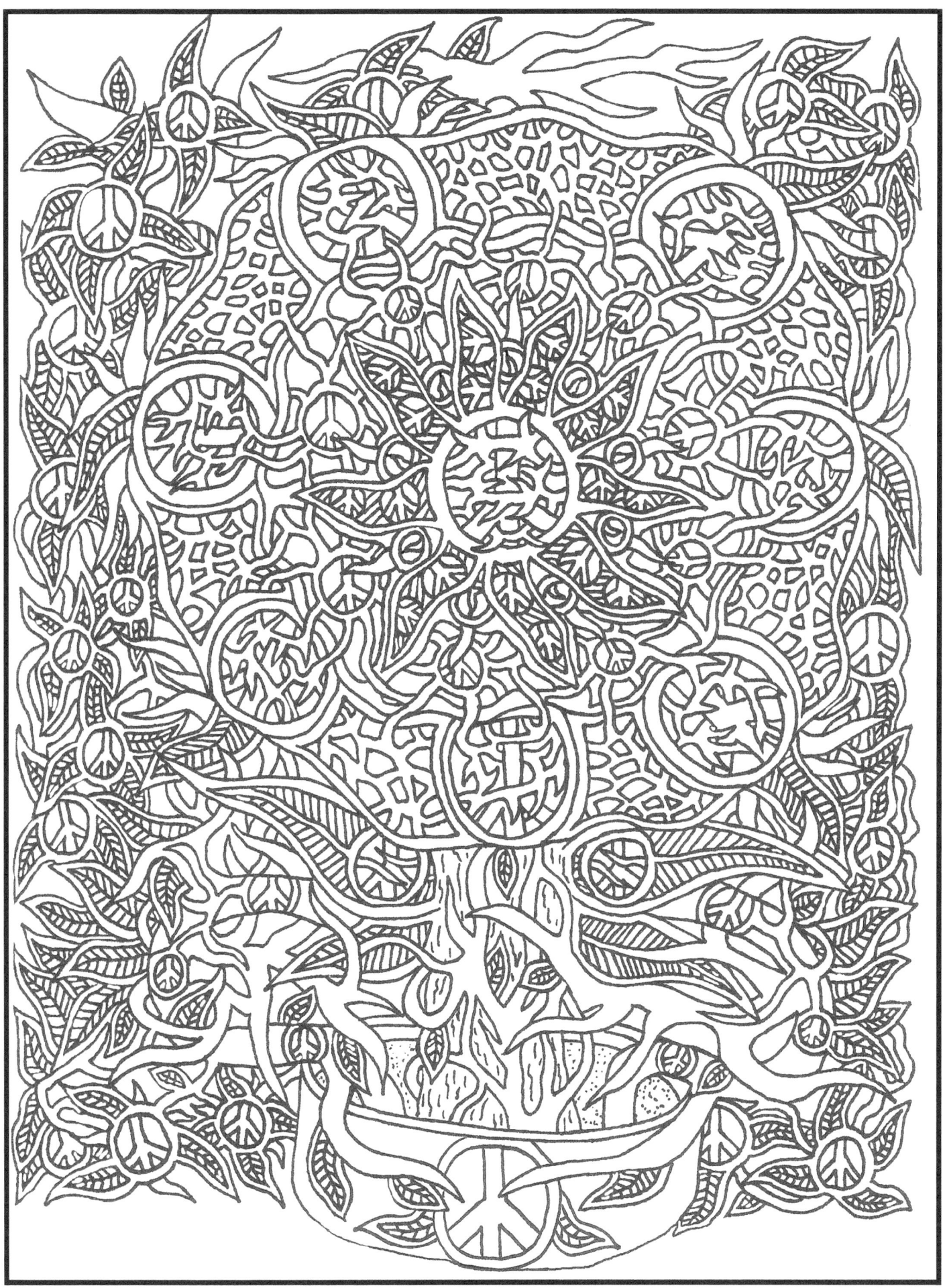

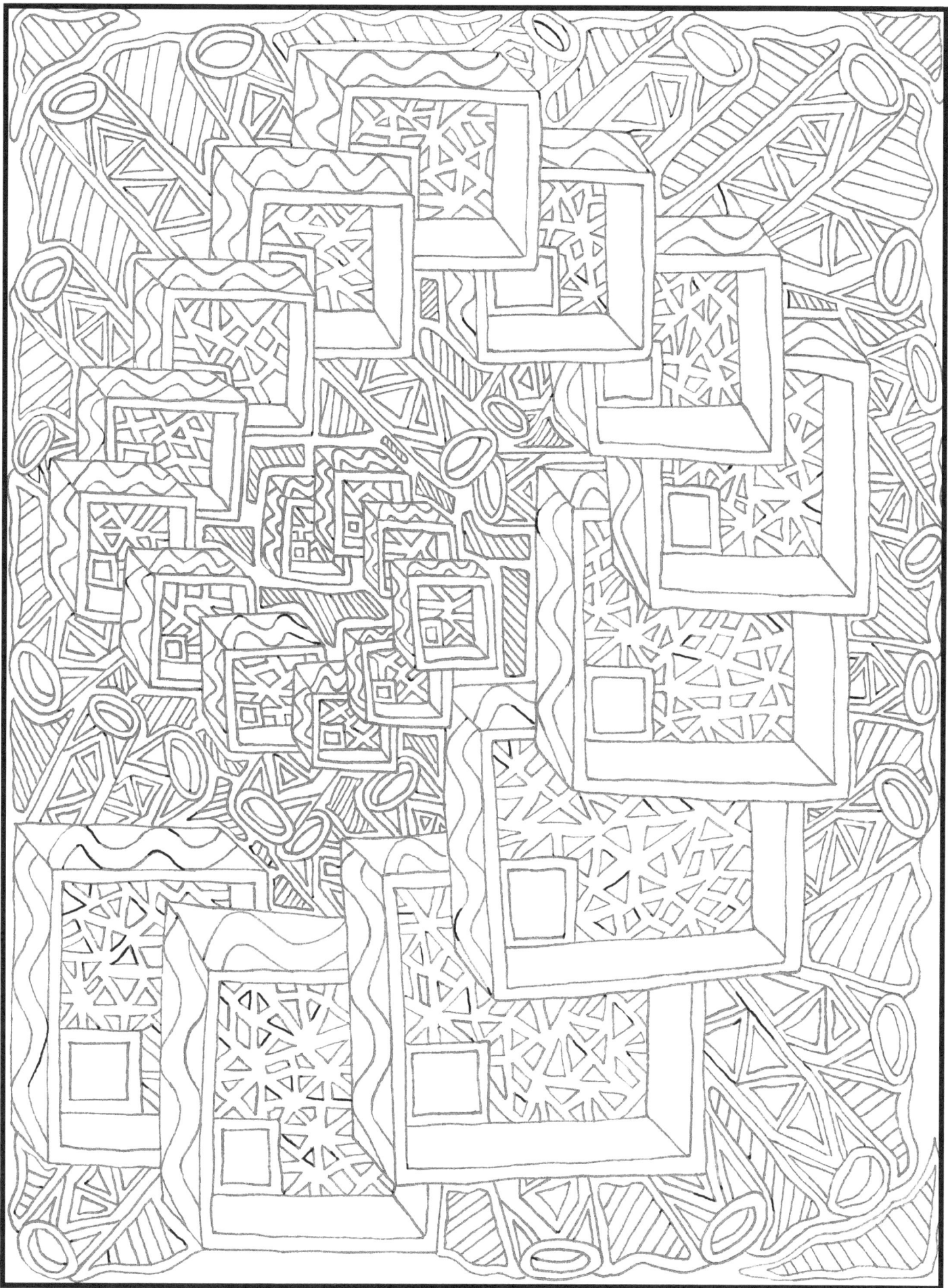

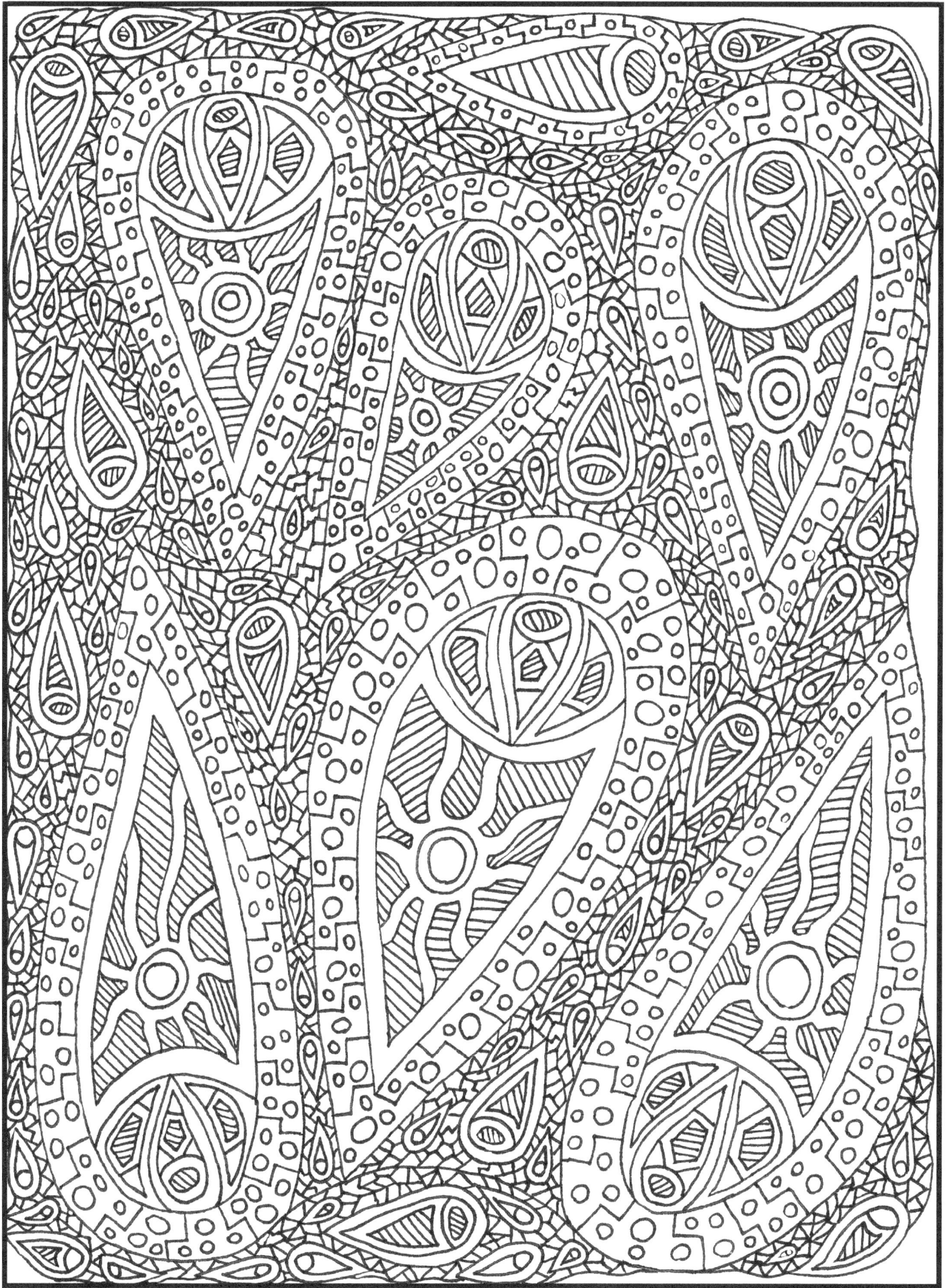

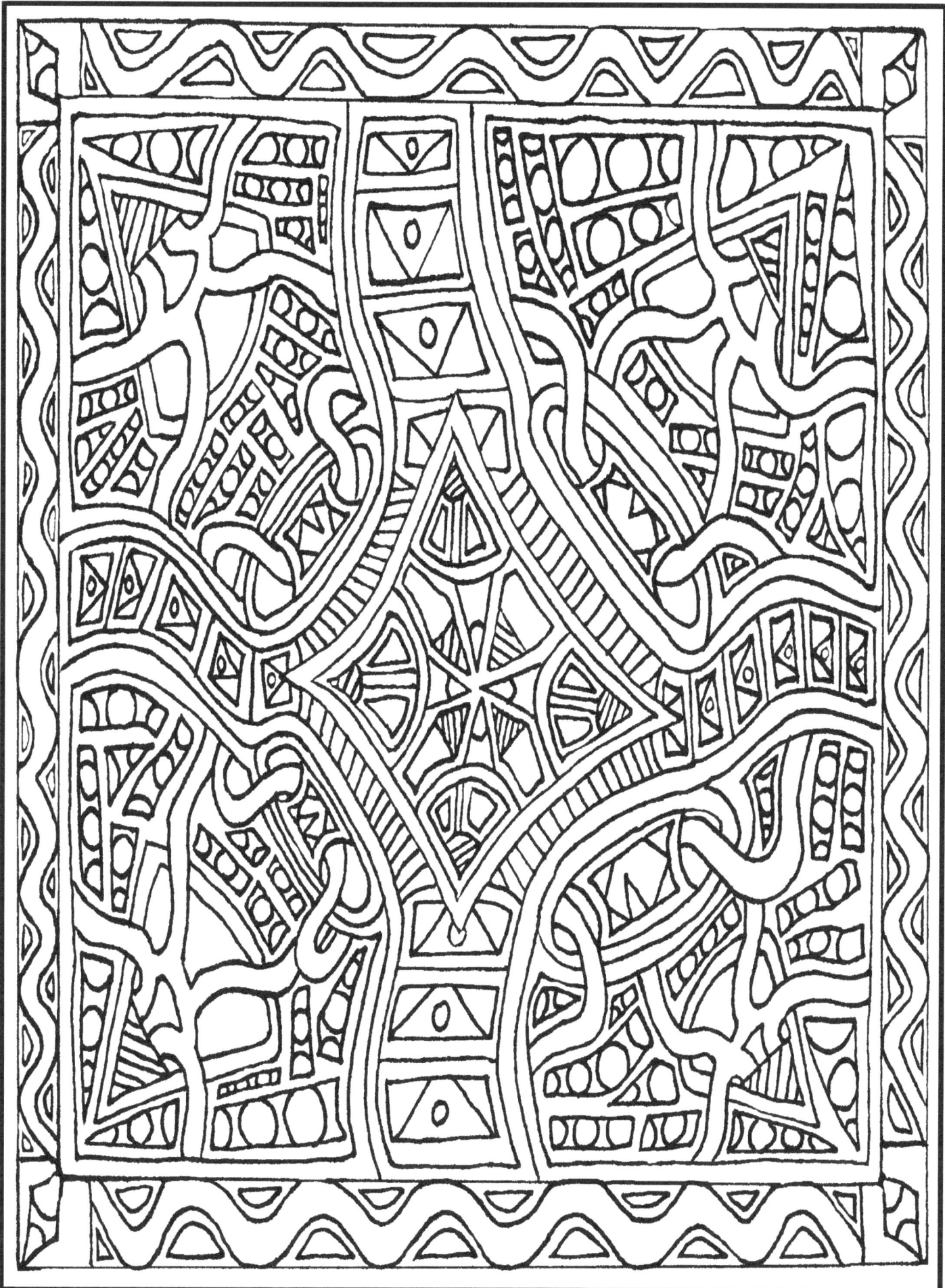

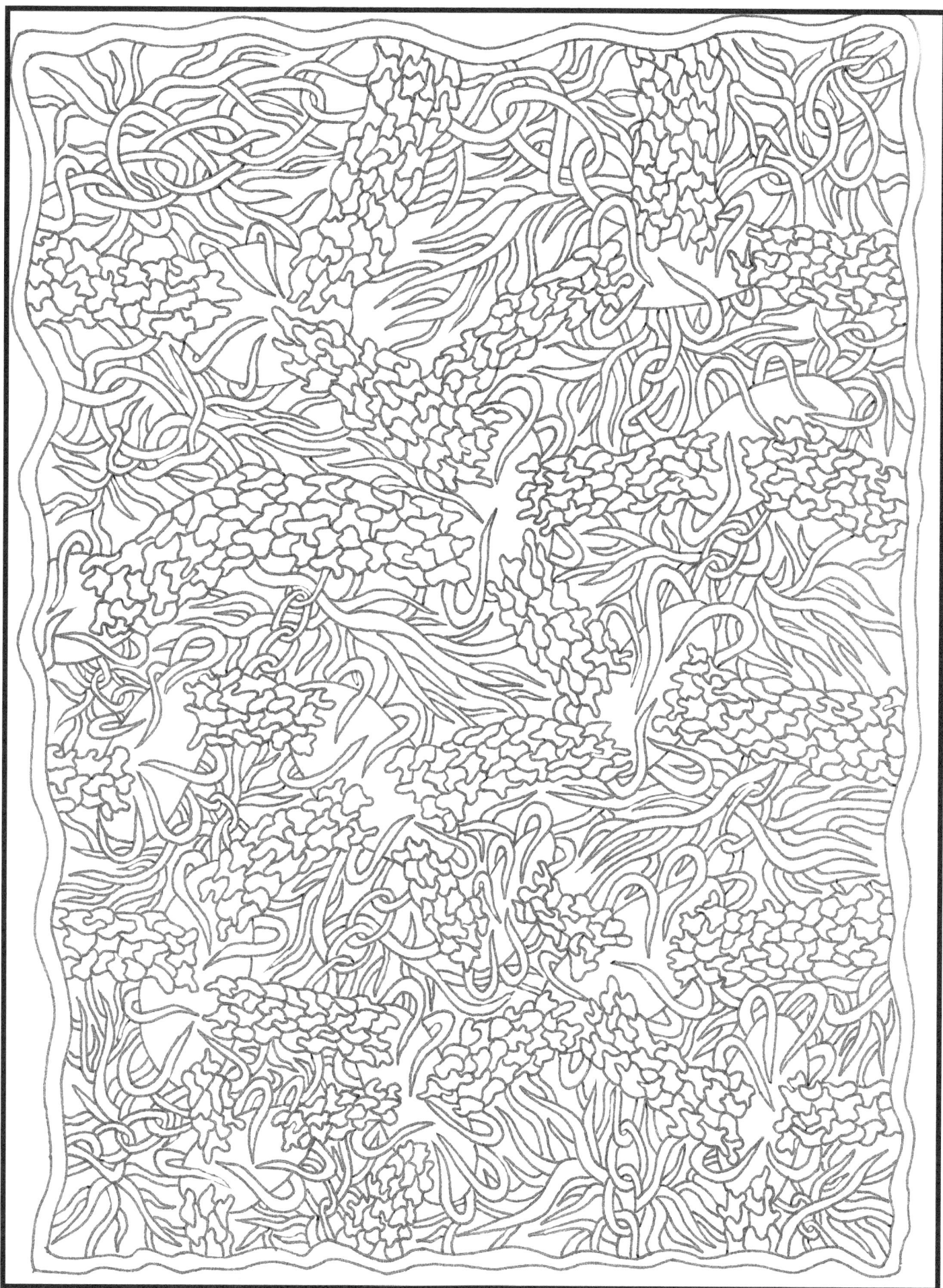

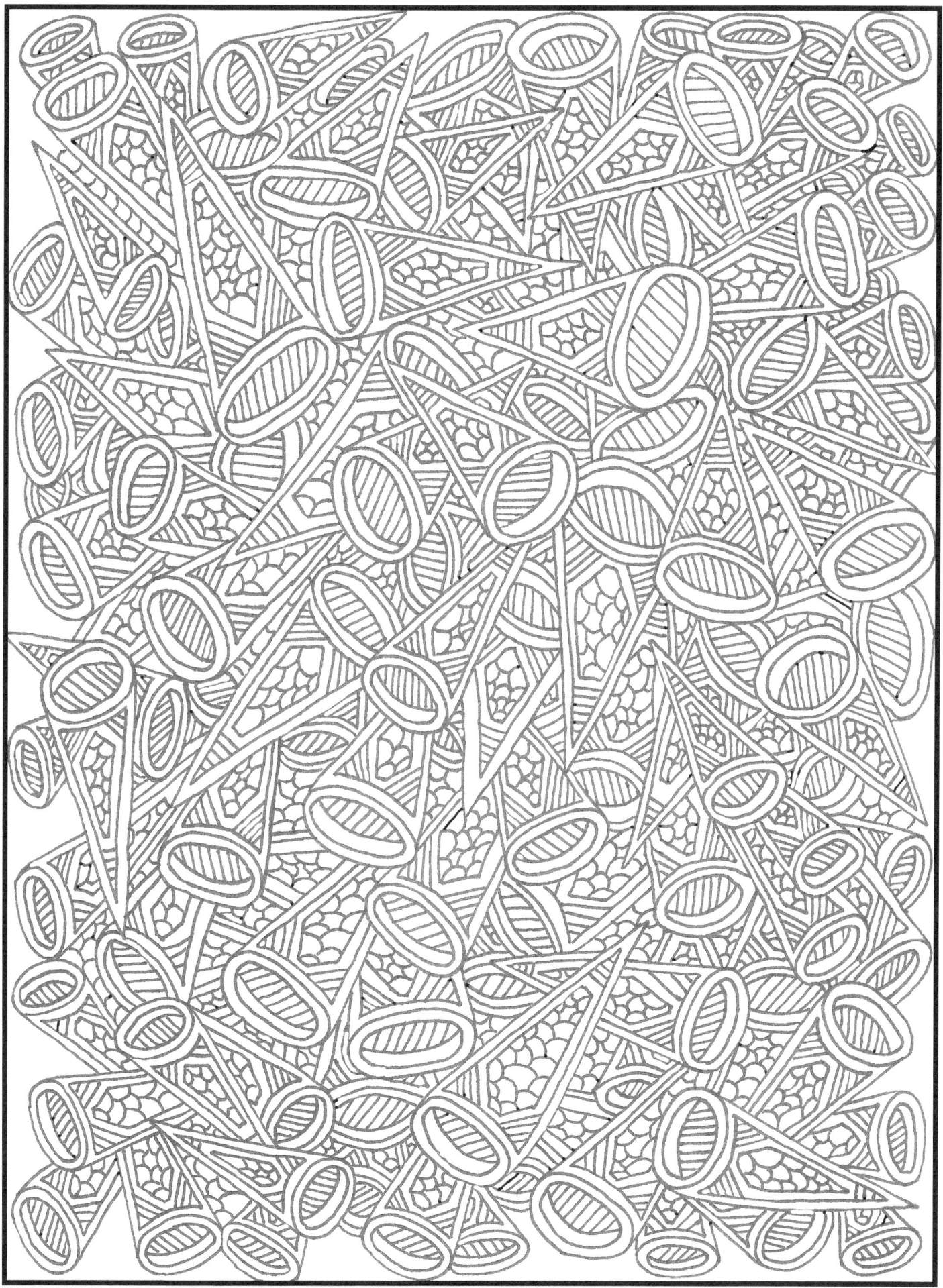

For more books
email me at damonehe@yahoo.com
or mail me at PO. box
2433 Newport Oregon
97365
or you can visit damonesart.com

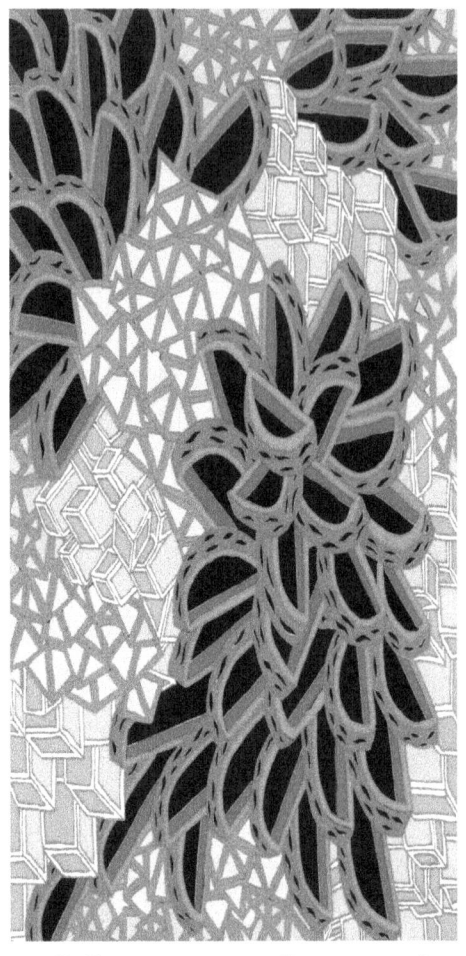
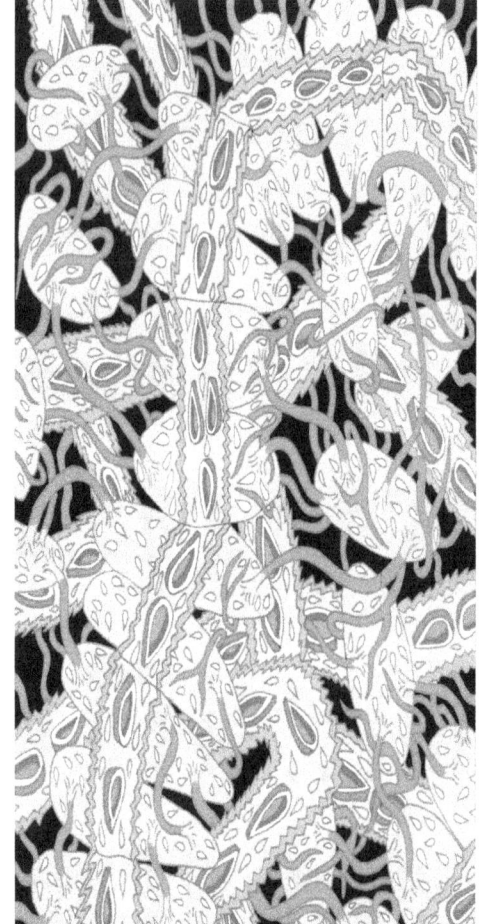
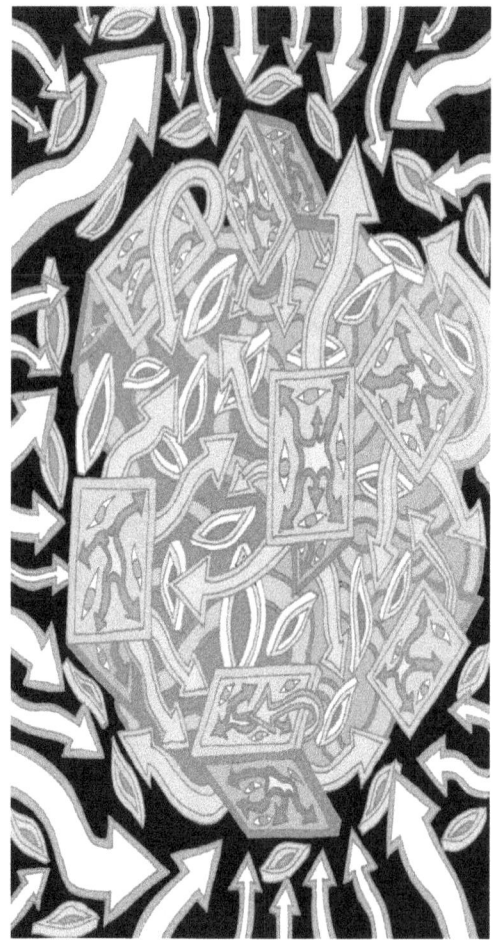

All Art done by Damone Heins

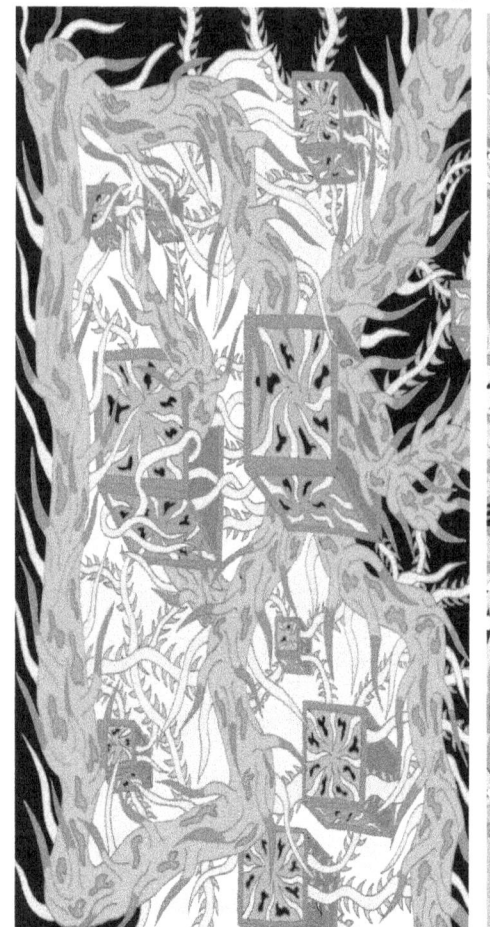
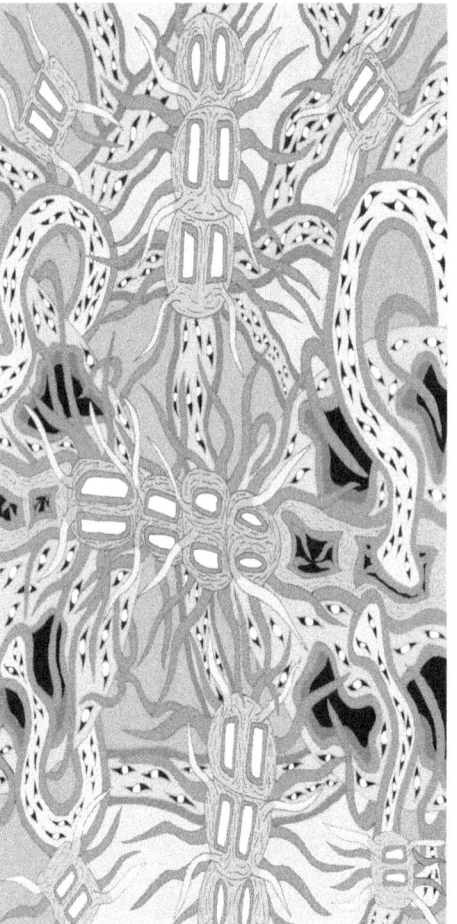
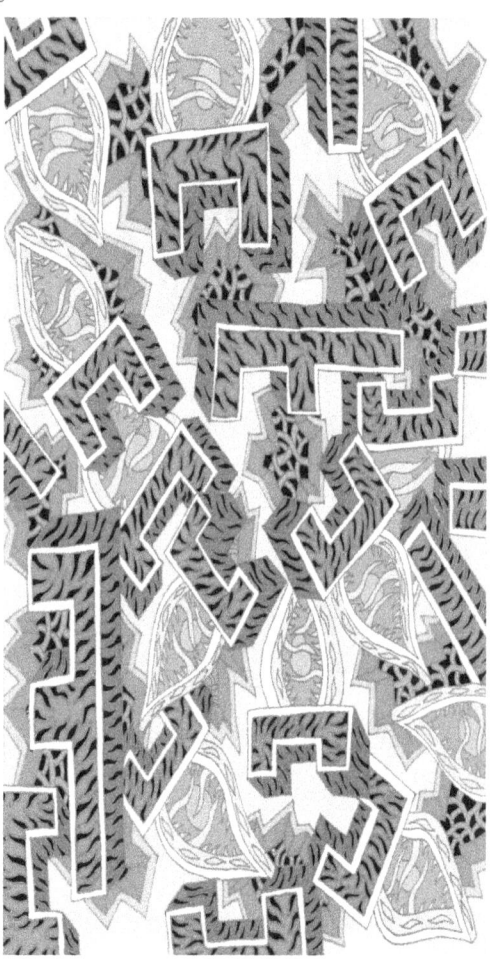